THE
ANTIDTE

Also Available by Chris:

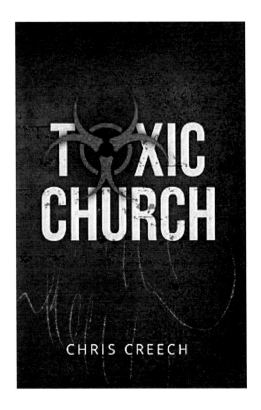

The ANTIDOTE Seminar Series in Video downlaod at toxicchurch.org.

THE
ANTID⊕TE

Real Biblical Cures for
T☣xic
Churches, Ministries, and Lives

CHRIS CREECH

The Antidote: Real Biblical Cures for Toxic Churches, Ministries and Lives

Copyright © 2018 Chris Creech
All Rights Reserved

ISBN 978-1-60225-007-9

ISBN (ebook) 978-1-60225-008-1

Cover and interior design: Motherhood Printing & Etc.

Published 2019

Motherhood Printing & Etc.
45973 Road 795
Ansley, NE 68814
http://motherhoodprinting.com

Printed in the United States of America

Dedicated to Jonathan Park, My Dear Korean Brother,
Whom I Pray is Doing Well After Enduring a Savage Attack at the
Hands of an Asian Antagonist.

Table of Contents

.

Preface

In 2006 my wife and I thought we had pastoral ministry figured out. We had served in ministry for thirty-two years, almost entirely in the role of senior pastor or church planters. I had a master of divinity and a Ph. D. from the largest and one of the most prestigious seminaries in the world. All of our churches had grown, sometimes quite dramatically. But despite this, we knew what it was like to be unfairly and viciously attacked by a few of the members of our churches. We knew what it was like to receive hate mail and hear lies about our ministry. However, we came to realize that we had much more to learn.

I was seeking support for our missionary service in Southeast Asia. So, I regularly visited pastors in the hope that their churches would support us. As I visited pastors, I came to realize the depth of suffering that many local pastors were enduring was far greater than that which we had experienced. It seemed that every time a pastor realized that I had considerable experience in ministry, he would begin to tell me the tragic details of how he was under attack. Over a dozen times, I talked to pastors who were very close to being forced out of their role as senior pastor. Each of these pastors was eventually either fired or forced to resign. One even died from a cancer that may have been related to the constant stress he endured in the pastorate. In fact, I came to accept the fact that many pastors were looking for help from someone. I was a safe person to hear their story since I was a missionary who would soon be leaving the US. So, they frequently shared their horror stories with me.

A time with one young pastor had a profound effect on our lives. I had an appointment with this pastor in a large American city. But when I went to the front door of his church, it was locked. I knocked, but no one came to the door. But there was one car in the parking lot.

So, I went around to other doors of the church. Eventually I found an unlocked door. The lights were off in the building. So, I began walking around, calling out to see if anyone was there. No answer! Then I came to a door that was slightly ajar and I heard something. I heard the sound of man who was weeping. I went into the unlit room, identified myself and asked if I could help. His sobbing continued. He then began to tell me his story. He was the pastor of the church and he was under attack from a group of people within the church. The lead attacker was the head of a para-church ministry in the area. As I listened to this pastor's story, I was struck by the depth and vicious nature of the attacks he was enduring. His story was one in which the evil he was enduring was much greater than anything we had experienced. I realized that this pastor was very near suicide! As a missionary raising support, I was not allowed to offer counsel. But I did listen for well over an hour. I put my arms around this man, like a father comforting a son and I prayed for him. I asked him to tell his story to a denominational leader. He agreed. I later learned that he did not tell anyone else his story. He resigned from his church. (This was probably the best solution for his situation.) But as I left the church that day, I realized this young man was experiencing more than mere attacks. People who called themselves Christians were attempting to destroy his life. I found myself praying in the car. "Lord, if you ever want me to do something to stop these horrible attacks, please lead me."

Then, we moved to Asia. We anticipated that the types of problems we had seen in the American church would not occur in Asia. The principal of the seminary immediately asked if I would serve the seminary as chaplain in addition to our regular duties as seminary lecturers. He knew of our ministry experience and thought we would be valuable in this position. And so, I became the chaplain and my wife became the "chaplette." But soon we realized there were deep problems in this Asian seminary among many of the students. As soon as the students learned that we loved them and their stories would remain confidential, a floodgate of stories came to our ears. Over and over again, we heard stories of abuse. This time the abuse was not as much about a leader being abused by followers. In Asian culture the problem is often one in which leaders abuse those in their charge. Within a few months of starting at the seminary, I found myself discussing the problem of the needs of the students with the principal. He informed me that the words "member care" (providing nurture for missionaries and people in ministry) did not exist within many Asian ministries. It was agreed that Faith and I would begin a class to help students deal with relational problems in ministry. I researched dozens of Christian books concerning the subject. I also began the process of interviewing pastors and missionaries from both Asia and the US. I also used considerable material that I had used in the past while discipling leaders. Slowly, a course began to take shape. The class was titled "Relationship Building for Life and Ministry." The course proved to be immensely popular among the students. The Biblical principles we were teaching were really helping students deal with the problem of abusive relationships within church and missionary ministry teams.

Then, what happened to one of the students became another pivotal event in our lives. A young Korean man was savagely attacked by one of the faculty members of the seminary. The seminary principal was on sabbatical in another country. Since the principal was absent, this faculty member seemed to feel the freedom to attack others. So, the faculty member had arranged the attack with the help of a couple of other enabling faculty members. The attack was totally unjust. But we were powerless to help. Since we were not Asians and not part of seminary leadership, our mission organization wisely advised us not to become involved. Shortly after the attack began, we found this young man waiting on our apartment stoop for us to come home from the seminary. He did not have an appointment, but he was desperate. We invited him in and had supper with him. He then began to share his story. He began to sob. Public emotion is something Asian men and particularly Koreans simply do not do. He had been badly shamed by this faculty member. Korean culture is a shame-based culture. Koreans have a somewhat surprising way to handle shame. They commit suicide. The method of choice is jumping off high buildings. Since we lived on the ninth floor of the apartment block, we were concerned. As he told us his story, he sat very near our balcony door which was open in order to allow a breeze to flow through the apartment. We listened for several hours. We prayed for him and I drove him home. His sobbing continued in my double-parked car for over another hour. He was begging for help, but I had been forbidden to do anything. I have never regretted any decision more than the one I made to do nothing to help this young friend. We really were powerless. My superiors were right. Any interference from us would have produced extensive problems. The attacking faculty member knew what was happening to this young man from a shame-based culture. This was an attack which was meant to destroy this young man's life.

The antagonistic faculty member attacked many other students. Then, the attacker began to attack my wife and I. Remember: The seminary principal was on sabbatical. Despite the fact that my wife and I were well loved by all of the faculty members except one and despite the fact that we were well loved by all of the students, my wife was told she was no longer needed as a help at the seminary. This was in violation of the agreement that had been made between the seminary and our mission sending organization. Neither my wife or I had said or done anything to interfere with what the attacker was doing to many of the students. No one had heard one word from us. However, likely the subjects of our class had offended the attacker. It was the end of our four-year term as missionaries. So, we returned home for a year of reporting to churches and individual supporters. When we left Asia, the young Korean man, who had been attacked, met us at the airport with a gift and hugs for both of us. He had been dismissed by the seminary, but he was grateful to us for the love that we had given to him. When the principal returned from sabbatical, he was dismissed by the seminary board for unwarranted reasons despite having served for over thirty years with the organization that had founded the seminary. How could this happen? One attacker had used a couple of unwitting faculty members while the other faculty members remained silent. When we returned to Asia, we had arranged to begin teaching at another seminary.

These events left their mark. From the course that we had been teaching, our first book, *Toxic Church*, was penned. But we have come to realize that *Toxic Church* did not complete the task of addressing the issue of abusive relationships within local churches and ministry teams.

In the years following the writing of *Toxic Church*, we have become aware of a strange disconnect that often occurs between those in Christian leadership and an understanding of this destructive problem. Those who have experienced abuse, either as ministry leaders or layman, get it. They are fixated on learning about the nature of the problem when they read our first book. However, those who have not experienced significant abuse often dismiss the problem, blaming the victims rather than the attackers. They are ambivalent toward the principles that are presented in *Toxic Church*. And not surprisingly, those who are a significant part of the problem, either as attackers or the enablers of attackers, attack the book and us whenever opportunity arises. This has only caused us to be more determined than ever to explain the nature of this problem and its solutions. Though only the Lord can open the eyes of many who refuse to consider this massive problem and its solutions, we will continue to do what we can to address this problem through prayer, teaching our course, and writing this and other books.

While in Asia during our second term, our course broadened. We began to address not only the cause, but also the Biblical solutions for abusive behavior within ministry circles. So, this book, *The Antidote*, has been written to reflect the additional material in our course. *The Antidote* includes not only further information about the causes of conflict and abuse within ministry teams, it also teaches the Biblical answers. It teaches the real, Biblical Antidote for these problems.

First, more in depth teaching regarding how Satan provokes attacks is included in *The Antidote*. This is necessary as it helps victims understand what causes the attacks that occur. Regularly, the victim is scapegoated by an attacker and his or her enablers within a ministry team or local church. Because the cries regarding the evil that the victim has done are so regularly heard, victims often come to believe the false charges against themselves. This is the reason many find themselves marked for life. They come away from attacks believing that the charges are true. They often believe they are flawed human beings who cannot be used by God in any way due to their own inherent, permanent dysfunction. However, when they learn the true nature of the attack and how the attack was provoked, they gain a perspective which allows them to correctly identify where they failed and, more importantly, where they did not fail.

The Antidote also teaches that with an understanding and application of a very simple, but vital Biblical Antidote, accompanying Biblical solutions can also be properly applied. Included in these accompanying solutions are the ability to correctly identify the true causes of a problem, the ability to properly apply Biblical confrontation to those who have enabled the problem, and an ability to properly disciple Christians so that these problems do not occur. I now invite you, the reader to look into the nature of conflict and abuse within local churches and many other ministry circles. I also invite you to learn how to Biblically address these problems which are so often a part of ministry. Please now give attention to The Antidote.

Chapter 1
R.B. and *The Antidote*

R. B. dominated Wildwood Church. He stood almost 6' 6" tall, weighing well over 350 pounds. Every inch of his large physique was muscle. He was a champion wrestler in college, and almost made the Olympic wrestling team. He had won every possible high school accolade in athletics. He was not only a champion wrestler; he had also been the best lineman on the football team and the center who brought a state championship to his high school basketball team. Now, he was the key leader of his hometown church, The Church in the Wildwood. Everything he said eventually overruled every other leader's ideas. His name was an abbreviation that his high school football team gave him: R. B. stood for Raging Bull! His name not only described his physique and his football prowess; it described everything about his behavior. His will was extremely difficult to resist. He controlled Wildwood Church.

Wildwood had been a strong, small-town church. The senior board of eight members was not only dominated by R. B., but several of the other members of the board were his close friends or family members. One of the members was his son, Bryan. Bryan looked very little like his father. He was just as tall as his father, but he was quite lean. In fact, he looked more like a human beanpole than a raging bull. The other members with the exception of three were dutifully obedient to everything R. B. suggested.

Then, a major conflict began to brew. The pastor of Wildwood, Pastor Harry, had been at the church for eight years. He was sixty years old. The church had not grown at all during Pastor Harry's tenure and a problem was looming. The average attendance had dropped from 250 to 125 in the eight years of Pastor Harry's leadership. It was evident to R. B. and several other key members of the board that Pastor Harry was doing as little as possible. It seemed that he would stay on as the pastor until his retirement. But the question was: Would the church survive another five or six years with Pastor Harry? Another factor was at work. The average age of the adults at Wildwood Church was between sixty-five and seventy. The number of funerals far exceeded the number of conversions. In fact, the baptismal tank hadn't been used for years for any purpose other than the baptism of those who had grown up in the church. Wildwood Church had a bleak future. Anyone could see that slow death was now in process at Wildwood.

It was time for R. B. to act. Through his tenacious efforts and the pressure he placed on the members of the board, Pastor Harry was asked to resign. However, Pastor Harry was dearly loved by many within the church, particularly the older members whom he constantly coddled. In fact, it appeared that the only thing Pastor Harry had ever done besides the obligatory preaching was to sit with the old folks and make them happy. Many of the members of the church were outraged, particularly the older ones. They called meeting after meeting where they stated their objections. They were to no avail. R. B. dug in his heels. Eventually, the meetings became more and more ugly. Some even stated that they hated R. B. and his "crew." Eventually, well over half of the members of the church left. Three members of the board also left the church.

The Church in the Wildwood became an empty shell of what it had been. Forty to fifty attenders were all that remained. R. B. had won, but the Church in the Wildwood had lost. Offerings dropped dramatically. There was no way the church could continue. There were barely enough funds to pay for building maintenance much less a new pastor.

My wife and I were called by a denominational leader to determine if there was anything we could do. We had the advantage of a highly trained and experienced interim pastor who was a professional counselor with over twenty-five years of pastoral experience. He had primed the church leaders for our possible interaction with them. We met with the five remaining members of the board. We noticed that two of the five questioned the decision to fire Pastor Harry. We suggested the only thing we could. We asked if they would meet with us for a ten-day period which would include eight evenings and all-day Saturday and half a day on Sunday. We described the program we would conduct. We would do something of an autopsy of the situation with recommendations to follow. They were open. The church was near death and even the board was questioning itself. There was no opposition, even from R. B. They were desperate. They knew they needed help.

We conducted our usual routine of lectures and small group meetings. I met with the members of the board for the small group meetings. All of them were male. My wife met with the wives of the board members for the same purpose. In the course of the small group meetings, we led these ten individuals into a program of self-discovery as to why they behaved the way they did and how this had affected the church. We eventually came to the time in which we began the process of exploring "The Antidote." It was at that time something very special happened. The small Sunday school room where I was meeting with the men suddenly changed. We could feel, in a palpable way, the presence of the Holy Spirit. As Bryan began to process The Antidote, he suddenly broke down into tears. At first, he sobbed. But, the sobs turned into something like a wail. He could barely talk. All he could do was call on the Lord for help! Then, it happened again, this time with another member of the board, Joe, who had been Bryan's close friend. Joe also began to sob. No voice was heard in the room for what seemed almost half an hour. Then, the dam broke. R. B. began to sob and weep like a baby. He began confessing sins—some of which were unknown by anyone in the room. Completing the exercises around The Antidote was unnecessary. The Holy Spirit had been there. He had changed everything. Wildwood was about to see a major revival.

The following Sunday worship service witnessed a dramatic healing. R. B. stood and began to confess publicly the sins of his life, including the sins that he had done which had destroyed Wildwood Church. He resigned from the board! Everyone was shocked. But, all around the room, individuals slowly stood to confess their own complicity in the problems of Wildwood Church. There was a new spirit within the church. All that remained was to seek what the Lord would ask the church to do to regain His blessing.

The story I have shared with you is true. Of course, I have changed the circumstances enough so that it is impossible to identify the church or its members. My wife and I really saw this happen. Today, Wildwood Church is again a strong church. Every Sunday the attendance grows. It may soon be a church of 150 again. The offerings are large enough to pay for the expenses including those needed for a pastor. Many of those who left Wildwood have returned. But new, young families are also beginning to attend. Conversions now occur and the baptismal tank is now being used again. The work of the interim pastor continues the process of the complete revitalization of Wildwood Church. He understands the concept of The Antidote and has made certain the concept is steadfastly promoted. R. B. is not a member of the board and may not ever be a board member again, but he is faithful! He attends; He gives financially and, he constantly demonstrates a servant heart. Most importantly, R. B. is being discipled by the interim pastor. R. B. is seeing the restoration of his life and ministry.

My wife and I have been blessed to see how the Lord used the simple, Biblical principle of The Antidote repeatedly, many, many times, both in the US and in many countries in Asia. The results have been remarkable. It is a not a complicated Biblical principle. But it is a principle which is overlooked and poorly applied over and over again. The result is that many Christians are prisoners to the problems which are programmed into their lives by the powers of evil. It is a remarkable lesson; for once this lesson has been learned, many of the problems and pains of this life cease to have any effect. Often, the way that God directs the life of the Christian through individual experiences is then understood. Often, why a Christian's hopes are fulfilled or remain unfulfilled is also understood. Often, why prayers are answered positively or negatively becomes clear. And often, the Christian who learns this lesson amazingly begins to understand the very nature of emotional pain; why it is there; and how much, if not all of it, can be eliminated. It is not too strong a statement to say that once the lesson of The Antidote is learned, many of the secrets of the truly abundant Christian life are realized. And, this lesson has one other, very positive effect: Once this lesson is understood there is a potential that all conflict will be eliminated within the life and the ministry of the individual Christian. In this sense, it is a true antidote to the poison of toxicity. It has the power to eliminate toxicity in relationships within every Christian ministry and within the life of every Christian.

Chapter 2
How To Use This Book

Even though the lesson of The Antidote is clearly taught in Scripture, it can be a difficult one to learn. Its application wars against the Christian's human nature. Normally, the Holy Spirit teaches each individual Christian this lesson through the Word of God and the experiences of life. But the lesson can also be learned by one Christian teaching another so long as the individual is willing to take radical steps to deny his or her own natural desires. If you, as the reader of this book, do not already know what The Antidote is, take heart. You can learn this lesson.

However, this book has a dual purpose. The first purpose is to help the reader understand The Antidote and other important lessons in the task of eliminating toxic relationships from within churches and ministry teams. The second purpose is to assist Christians who want to help others learn these lessons. This book is actually a simple blueprint for teaching the course about The Antidote. This course has been taught in seminaries, churches, missions and para-church organizations in many parts of the world with the result that over eighty percent of those who take this course gain significant insight into the ways that the Lord is working in their lives. They are thus able to adjust their goals and hopes, complying with the will of God. As the reader goes through the chapters, he or she is actually reading through the lectures of the course. These lectures can then be taught in ways that help others to apply these life-changing lessons to their own lives.

However, the course is not designed to be taught only with the lectures that are contained in the chapters of this book. How the primary lessons of this book are applied to each person differ according to the personality and life experiences of each Christian.

Individualized plans for the application of these lessons are necessary. At the end of the book is a series of exercises that are designed to be used within small group settings of three or four students and one facilitator. The purpose of these exercises is to help the student design the particular application of the central lesson of this book to his or her life in an individualized manner. The small group sessions are designed to be interspersed in between the lectures. The general format is one in which each lecture of about three hours is followed by a small group meeting of about three to four hours. As the book proceeds through the lectures of the course, the approximate progress that the student should complete in the exercises will also be suggested. I am deeply indebted to the material presented by Minirth, Meier, and Hemfelt, particularly in their book, *Love is a Choice* in the design of these exercises. Though these exercises have been significantly amended over the years, the Minirth and Meier studies provided a wonderful beginning for the small group exercises that have been used. These small groups should separate men and women for obvious reasons. If a group consists of less than three individuals and a facilitator, it is possible that insights will be missed by those who are seeking to help one another. There may not be enough interaction to help a member of the small group in the task of designing a plan for the application of the lessons from the course. However, if a group consists of more than four individuals and a facilitator, it is also possible that the group may be unable to come to insights for each individual. The length of time required to do the exercises may prevent suitable examination of each individual's life. Before an individual is allowed to participate in these groups, he or she should sign a statement regarding confidentiality and a willingness to assist others in the answering of the questions that are presented in each small group session. A suggested confidentiality statement is included in the appendix. This appendix also includes these exercises and instructions regarding how to use them. The purpose of these small groups and the small group exercises will become obvious as the reader examines the lectures that are contained in the chapters of this book. The goal of the lectures and the small groups is designed to coalesce in each participant's life at the end of the course with the application of The Antidote and related lessons in an individualized manner. The desired result is peace in the individual Christian's life and within his or her ministry. The appendix also includes a local church survey useful for analyzing the potential for conflict within any local church or Christian ministry.

Something else of importance should be mentioned. At times, serious issues can surface as individuals go through these small group exercises. Thus, trained Christian counselors should be made available for individualized help when needed. A facilitator may suggest a professional Christian counselor for an individual rather than continuing with the small group. This possibility should be mentioned to each individual within the small group during the first small group session. Though this is a rare possibility, it can occur. A facilitator must be aware of varying levels of need. The goal is to help each person apply the central, life-changing lesson of The Antidote.

Before beginning the lectures of the course, the writer has a simple request: Please read my first book on this subject, *Toxic Church*. This first book describes the depth of the problem of ministry conflict. It also presents an elemental understanding of why conflict occurs. This second book will add further Biblical material regarding the fundamental cause of conflict and toxicity within ministry circles. To fully understand this second book, a basic understanding of the principles from the first book will be helpful. The first book also presents some of the solutions for the problem of conflict. In this second book, more is added from Scripture regarding the solutions for toxic problems within ministry circles.

It is now time to turn the page, to begin to unravel the mystery of conflict and see the simple, Biblical and sometimes radical solutions to the problem. Let us begin this study by considering how Scripture describes the genesis of the human problem and the cause of relational conflict. This is something of a review of the material from *Toxic Church*, but it does contain some noticeable new references from Scripture and more, in-depth understanding of the human problem. These new references and understandings are the basis for the key lesson of this book, *The Antidote*.

Part 1
The Fall and What it Does to Human Relationships

"...,visiting the iniquity of the fathers on the children, on the third and fourth generation of those who hate Me," Exodus 20:5b

Chapter 3
It All Started With Adam

Adam and Eve really lived. One of the ways to prove their existence is the fact that the same mitochondrial DNA from one particular woman exists within every human being who has ever lived. Science proves that this can only have occurred if one woman is the mother of all humans. There are other ways to confirm Adam and Eve's existence. But what is perhaps the greatest confirmation of their existence, is the fact that the human condition can be understood by examining the events surrounding these two individuals. There is no other way to explain why we experience so much pain in this life.

Genesis 2:25 describes a very important fact about the condition of Adam and Eve. They were naked and yet unashamed. This simple statement has enormous implications. This means that they were complete in the knowledge that they had no need to validate or justify their own existence. They were secure in themselves without having to do one thing. This provided enormous freedom for the two of them. There was no need, of any kind, to seek acceptance from each other. They felt acceptable the way they had been created.

This was about to change. In Genesis 2:16–17, Adam was given a command from God not to eat from one particular, forbidden tree. What is important to note is that at the time in which the command was given, Eve had not yet been created. The creation of Eve is described in Genesis 2:18–24. She did not hear this original command. The command contained only one injunction: Don't eat of one particular tree.

A problem concerning this command is revealed in Genesis 3. In Genesis 3:1, the Serpent asked Eve what the command of God was. The Hebrew language of the text indicates very clearly that the Serpent was none other than Satan. However, the question was not a particularly devious statement, just a simple question. At this point, all that Satan was doing was just asking a question, "What does the Word of God say?" What Eve stated in Genesis 3:2–3 was the crux of the problem. Eve added three words to the command given to Adam: These three words were "or touch it." She stated that it was wrong not only to eat of the tree, but also to touch the tree. She added that the result would be death. These three words, "or touch it," were critical as they inferred that God had created something that was unsafe to touch. They were not in the original command. So, the question must be asked, "Where did Eve get this misunderstanding?" There are only two possibilities. One is that she invented these three words? The other is that Adam misinformed her? We don't know which possibility is right. But, we do know one thing: Adam was there when the command was given and Eve was not. Therefore, Adam was definitely more responsible for her misunderstanding.

But realize what this means. Eve may have believed there was something wrong with the tree itself and not just something wrong with the command not to eat of it. Touching it produced death. And since God had created it, He was capable of creating a bad thing which could produce death. The words, "or touch it" suggest a serious misunderstanding on Eve's part. She believed God was capable of doing evil for He had created something that had the capacity to produce pain. In other words, she saw the problem was not simply one of obedience to God. It was one in which an evil god had created something which could produce pain, for this god had created an evil thing.

The Serpent in Genesis 3:4–5 then simply questioned her understanding by stating that God knew she would not die. The Serpent added that God knew that eating from the tree would provide special knowledge, a knowledge like that which God possessed for she would then know the difference between good and evil. Thus, Eve, who had already questioned the goodness of God in the act of creating the tree, was confronted with a second possible evil motive of God. He wanted to prevent her from gaining some special knowledge. Now, Eve already knew the difference between good and evil. She knew that it was good not to eat from the tree and evil to eat from it. However, she did not know something very important.

She did not possess the knowledge or the experience of what would happen if she were to eat of the tree. If a mother tells a child not to touch a hot stove, the child knows it is right not to touch the stove and wrong to touch it. But the child doesn't know what touching the hot stove does. Further knowledge is tied to the hot stove. It is called burned fingers. So, what Satan is telling Eve is totally true. He is not lying to her. She will gain knowledge, but oh what a useless, painful knowledge.

Thus, Eve, having already questioned the goodness of God and possibly believing that God was hiding special knowledge from her, saw that the fruit of the tree was a delight to the eyes (Genesis 3:6). She accepted the statement that it would make her wise. So, she took of the tree and ate. But understand the process that goes with the eating of the fruit. She had to touch the tree or the fruit before eating it. Therefore, confirmation of the supposed truth which the Snake had given to her was completed. She was able to touch the tree without dying. Therefore, since touching seemingly had no serious consequence, eating would also have no consequence and possibly a great benefit. Thus, it appeared to Eve that the only consequence was that she would gain knowledge, something which she believed was good. So, she ate.

Then, she gave the fruit to Adam and he ate. Notice: Eve had an excuse. She misunderstood the command. She had been tricked. Adam had no such excuse. He just ate. He was not tricked in any way. And notice, Adam was "with her" as we see in verse 6. He was likely right there when she was being tricked by the Snake. Why didn't he correct her misunderstanding immediately after she stated it? Why didn't he take steps to prevent what happened? And where was the Serpent? Was he possibly in the tree, touching it? For that would demonstrate that the touching of the tree had no consequence as the Snake was able to touch the tree without penalty.

Then, the story became much more complicated in Genesis 3:7. They both realized they were naked. For the first time, they felt that the condition in which they had been created had to be covered. Something was not adequate about themselves in their own natural condition. They didn't like themselves; they were naked; they had to cover up! Their value no longer came just from existing. They had to "do" something to make themselves acceptable. They had to cover themselves. So, the knowledge which the Snake had suggested had now become real; there really were burned fingers that resulted.

This has enormous implications. They no longer liked themselves in their inherent condition. Psychologists have a fancy term for this condition. It is called "bad self-image." And we have all inherited a bad self-image from Adam and Eve. In the same way that we have inherited the color of our eyes or skin or some personality characteristic from our parents, we have also inherited from Adam and Eve the sense that we are somehow unacceptable. The way we know this is simple: We all wear clothes! We all believe we need to cover up. Why? Aren't we created by God in a perfectly whole condition? We are so affected by this development that even to ask why we need to clothe ourselves seems very strange.

But realize what this means. Since we no longer believe we have value in our natural condition, we question our own value. We see ourselves as inadequate and unacceptable and we must find a way to correct this unacceptability. This leads to subtly entering into the mindset of believing our value comes because of something we can "do" rather than on the basis of who we are! If I have no value because of who I am, there is no other way for me to prove my value other than by "doing" something. And so, we begin to search for something, anything we can do or perform to give us a sense of importance or value. We begin the search by considering some of our own abilities. Our athletic ability or our personal beauty or our scholarly aptitude become very important to us as they may distinguish us from others and help us win acceptance from others. Any human ability or talent becomes the compensating act which can be used to help a person discover the source of his or her needed sense of value. Even becoming a great artist, a great musician or a great craftsman takes on new meaning. Our daily work also becomes a source for our value. Every act must be done to prove one's own importance because deep down inside each person doubts his or her own value. And, because we doubt our own value, there is another reality. We all have a hidden fear, a little voice which cries out deep within us, "Won't someone love me? Won't someone notice me? What can I "do" to get someone to notice me? What can I "do" to make myself acceptable?"

As we age, the attempts to gain acceptance and recognition can change. If we have found value because of athletic ability or looks, aging slowly dissipates the ability to find value on the basis of these attributes. The real purpose we have is to control the response of others who may give us greater acceptance. When looks or other abilities no longer attain a positive response from others, we resort to baser attempts to control them. Many different tactics can be used. As an example, anger and critical spirit may appear. If I can prove myself more valuable than others through criticism, greater recognition may be achieved. If I lose my temper, I may gain greater recognition. Shouting always gets greater attention. A person can even feign pain or depression in the attempt to gain recognition. After all, if I am hurting, others will certainly give me more attention as they attempt to limit my pain. We may also find ourselves doing everything possible to gain control of others in the workplace or in the local church. Leadership positions become the all-consuming passion of a person's life. I can then say to myself you can't say I am unimportant because you have to do what I say. Money, of course, takes on much greater meaning because possessing money means I can gain control of others. Wealth always draws attention. And if a person has wealth or power, I can always say to myself that no one can say I'm not important; I'm important because I have money. Thus, earning money, hoarding money, spending money and gambling money take on extreme importance. In fact, money fixations are often the determiner of other, more serious dysfunctions.

The potential is now ripe for seeing others as a challenge in the task of gaining acceptance. The pretty little girl sees other pretty little girls as potential rivals who can seize the prize of acceptance by gaining too much attention. So, the pretty little girl demeans others whom she judges as not as pretty. Rivals are criticized and relegated to the position of being less important. In the same way, the athletic little boy sees other little boys as rivals who can steal the prize of taking what is seen as "my attention." These rivals must be defeated in some way in order to prevent them from taking the prize of attention and acceptance. The less athletic little boys are teased and given less acceptance. The concept of my school, my football team, my club or my country is touted as being better than the clubs or countries of others.

The inevitable result is conflict. Giving acceptance to another for a particular ability is seen as a threat to one's own ability to gain acceptance for that same ability. Acceptance must be taken from others in the attempt to compensate for the lack of attention which is constantly felt due to one's own human condition. So, a person gives acceptance to no one for anything. Critical spirit and demeaning others becomes standard behavior. A person believes that to belittle the achievements of others makes his or her own achievements and success more important. In addition, the need to control others becomes paramount. Insuring others are seen as less important is best accomplished by making certain they are subservient. A person says to himself, "No one can say I am unimportant if others do what I demand that they do." Thus, techniques to control others are developed including emotional rage, withholding acceptance, critical spirit, or feigning tears and pain. The inevitable result of all of this is rivalries, conflict and constant attempts to gain greater attention. Rather than being able to love others, this problem causes all of us to find ways to use others, all in the attempt to gain needed attention and acceptance.

Another result of doubting our own value is an inability to admit our own failings. After all, if I admit that I have done something wrong, I lose the ability to gain acceptance. So, I simply must find a way to deny my own wrongdoing. This is what happened in the continuing story of Adam and Eve. In Genesis 3:8–12, the two heard God walking in the garden and they hid themselves from Him. Not only were they unable to accept themselves the way they were; they also saw themselves as unacceptable in the eyes of others, in this case the eyes of God. Then, God asked Adam, "Where are you?" Now, why did God ask this question? Is it possible that He did not know where Adam was? Of course not! God knows everything. So, why did God ask this question? Adam replied that he knew he was naked and he was afraid. So, he hid himself. Then, God asked some other questions: "Who told you that you were naked? Have you eaten of the forbidden tree?" Now, once again, why did God ask these questions? Did He not know the answers? Then, one of the most troubling events in the entire story is Genesis 3:12. Adam answered by stating that the woman, whom God gave to be with him, gave him the fruit and he ate. In other words, Adam stated, "It's not my fault. She made me do it. And because you gave her to me, you made me do it." Everyone was responsible said Adam, except Adam.

Adam's actions were predictable. Because he was controlled by his need to prove his value on the basis of something he could do, he couldn't admit he was doing anything wrong. To do so risked his ability to find value on the basis of performance. So, he would logically say to himself that he couldn't do anything that is wrong and if he did do something wrong, he had to deny it. So, Adam found himself doing something that was truly despicable: blaming his wife for something he had done. He was the one who was responsible for Eve's misunderstanding of the command, not Eve! Eve had been given to him as a gift for it was not good for a man to be alone (Genesis 2:18). She was so important that Adam was supposed to leave his father and his mother and cleave to his wife (Genesis 2:24). Now, the woman who was to be cherished and loved by Adam was being victimized by Adam. This is the first example of one human hurting another. Adam's thought process was working in a strange way: Picture a large balance scale in your mind. (In the seminar I hold my arms out like the wings of an airplane to demonstrate what a balance scale looks like.) The balance scale is a picture of how our conscience works. If I do something wrong, one side of the scale is weighed down with a weight, called sin. (I dip one of my arms and raise the other arm to demonstrate the weight of sin.) I have two ways of bringing the scale into balance. I can admit what I have done and ask for forgiveness. This will remove the weight from one side of the balance scale. Or, I can put weight on the other side of the balance scale and bring the scale back into balance. (I move my arms appropriately into balance.) The weight on the other side is blaming someone else. This is what Adam did! Adam balanced the scale by blaming Eve. He balanced the weight on one side of the scale by putting weight on the other side of the scale. Because Adam doubted his own value, he had to prove that he had "done" nothing wrong. He did this by victimizing both Eve and God.

But, the problem of conflict and pain was furthered with these actions. How would Eve feel at this moment? She had been deceived by the Serpent. Adam had not. And Adam had been the one who had not adequately taught Eve about the command. He was the reason she was deceived. He was with her when she was deceived and did nothing to prevent it from happening. Now, he was blaming her when he, himself was the real culprit. What a despicable act. This dramatic injustice would produce in Eve what injustice always produces: Anger! Though the text does not give us this detail, it is logical to believe that Eve was angry, bitter and very hurt, undoubtedly to the point of tears and great emotional pain. Likely, the relationship between Eve and her husband has been harmed significantly and perhaps forever. Could she ever trust him again? Would there not be a barrier between the two of them from that day forward? It is doubtful that there was peace in the cave that night!

Now, add something else to what is happening in this scene. When God asked where Adam was and whether he had eaten of the tree, the Lord knew the answer. So, why did He ask? Because 1 John 1:9 tells us that God forgives when we confess. We also know that Malachi 3:6 tells us that God never changes. This means that if God forgives if we confess our sins today, He would also have forgiven Adam in that day. All Adam had to do was accept God's forgiveness. All he had to do was say "yes" when God asked if he had eaten from the forbidden tree. But due to his need to prove his value on the basis of something he could do or not do, he chose to scapegoat his wife and God. God was offering Adam forgiveness when He asked those three simple questions. He wasn't wondering where Adam was or who told him he was naked or whether he had eaten of the forbidden fruit. He was giving Adam a chance to confess. Unfortunately, Eve, also controlled by the need to find value on the basis of performance, followed in like manner, blaming the Serpent (who was actually quite culpable). However, this did not excuse Eve's action for she did eat of the forbidden fruit.

This was also the first time the concept of the "identified patient" became evident. Counselors and therapists know that when someone is brought for counseling, the likelihood is greater than 50% that the person who needs the counseling is not the person who is brought.

Rather, it is the person who did the bringing. The person who is the "identified patient" is likely not the real patient. The identified patient is the merely the convenient scapegoat. This is what Adam did with Eve. He made her the scapegoat, the "identified patient" by blaming her for the sin that he had done.

From that time until this, man has been faced with a question. When any of us do something that is wrong, we must decide whether we will confess our sin or excuse ourselves by blaming someone else or some circumstance. All humans are natural excuse-makers. But, the consequence of wrong doing is not only that we feel naked and doubt our own self-worth. We also can pass the blame onto someone else in the same manner as Adam. We do this by blaming members of our families or ministries or anyone around us by accusing someone else when we ourselves are the ones who have done wrong. And when we blame someone else, we add to our own sense of inadequacy. Passing the blame to another only worsens the problem. Adam knew, deep down inside, that he had done wrong. His act of blaming his wife only worsened the problem for now he not only felt guilt for the act of eating the forbidden fruit, but he also felt guilt for failing to accept his own culpability and blaming poor Eve.

This process affects each one of us because we are all subject to valuing ourselves on the basis of performance. The result is ever increasing pain and the need to find acceptance. This pain is called "love hunger" by counselors and therapists. We all have love hunger. We all know we are naked, incomplete in some way. We all attempt to find a way to compensate for this lack of acceptability by "doing" something. And we all find it difficult to accept our own wrong doing for as we accept our wrongdoing, we also risk losing acceptance. Thus, we all have a natural tendency to blame others and to make excuses should we fail in some way. Due to these tendencies, we all find ourselves constantly subject to emotional pain and the forces that produce conflict and separation from those around us. What a dismal situation! But, it gets worse!

Chapter 4
Adam Was Only the Beginning

In *Toxic Church*, I explain a process, commonly recognized in Christian counseling, which leads to generational dysfunction. This process is called the abuse cycle. The first step of the abuse cycle is the love hunger that is explained in Genesis 3. But the next steps in the abuse cycle begin to ensure that the problem of dysfunction and pain will worsen. The second part of the abuse cycle is called "magical thinking." Magical thinking is the process in which a child tries to win the favor of his or her parents or primary caregivers in an attempt to overcome the lack of love that comes from love hunger. It is the child's first attempt to "do" something to win the love that is missing. Children always believe that their parents or caregivers are perfect. Therefore, children believe that if they are not receiving enough attention or love from a parent or caregiver, the problem must be within their own behavior. To overcome this problem, children begin to try to "do" something, anything which magically causes a parent or caregiver to give the child more love.

Children are very intelligent. They know what pleases daddy or mommy. If daddy is a sports fan, that child will attempt to do athletic things to win daddy's favor. And when daddy is a sports fan, any athletic activity on the part of a child will result in greater attention from daddy. If a mother is a beautiful woman or if the child is complimented for wearing the right clothing or dressing the right way, the child will attempt to do the things which will bring attention for beauty. As an example of magical thinking, a child may say to himself or herself that if I am more fun to be around, daddy will give me more attention. And, there may be more attention given for behaving in a favorable way. Thus, the behavior of the child is reinforced. The child is being taught to seek love by performing or "doing" the right things. There is no limit to the ways the child can magically think they can win enough favor to cover the missing love that is in his or her life. Whatever the child believes will please daddy or mommy or any primary caregiver becomes the principle means that the child uses to win love and acceptance throughout life.

The account of Cain and Abel in Genesis 4:1–5 is a perfect example of magical thinking. Both Cain and Abel brought an offering to the Lord. Jude 11 and 1 John 3:12 describe Abel's offering as an example of righteousness whereas Cain's was regarded as evil. The original readers understood why Abel's offering was acceptable and why Cain's was not. The culture of that time understood perfectly the concept of animal sacrifice. This was what Moses was teaching in the first five books of the Bible. Why was Abel's animal sacrifice acceptable to God? Because it was a picture of the coming sacrifice of Jesus, first mentioned in Genesis 3:15. It was the act of Abel which stated in a concrete way that he was not acceptable. Through the sacrifice, he was saying he could not "do" anything to win acceptance. He needed the help of God. He needed the coming sacrifice of Jesus. He needed God to "do" something. Cain's sacrifice was different. He was attempting to produce his acceptance on the basis of his own "doing" and not the "doing" of God. He brought the produce of his hands. He was saying that he could "do" something without God's help. Thus, his act was an example of magical thinking. He thought that if he could just "do" the right thing, he would win the favor of God. It didn't work.

The problem with magical thinking is that it never works. As an example, a child will never be able to gain more time from a father who is addicted to work. The child simply doesn't have the power to change a workaholic father. The same is true of any attempt at gaining love through doing something. Even though a child may believe they have the magical ability to gain enough attention and love, these attempts always fail. The circumstance of not receiving enough attention simply cannot be corrected by the behavior of the child. The child simply does not have the power that he or she hopes. It is only magic, an illusion that will inevitably fail.

The third stage of the abuse cycle may then become apparent. It is depression. The story of Cain and Abel shows the problem of depression in Cain's life. In Genesis 4:5 we are told that Cain's countenance fell. This is a Biblical euphemism meaning that Cain became depressed. In Genesis 4:6–7, God told Cain that if he did well his countenance would be lifted up. Here is what happens within our conscience when we don't do something we should do. When we do wrong, the balance scale within our heads is pushed out of balance by the weight of the sin. (Remember the example of the arms being held upright to either side.) We can balance the scale by confessing or by putting weight on the other side of the scale by blaming another person. But there is another alternative. A person with an out of balance scale within his conscience can also blame and punish himself or herself through the act of producing depression. Depression punishes the person for what he or she believes has been done wrong and overcomes the problem of a balance scale that is out of balance. Depression is the act of punishing one's self for perceived or real wrong doing. It places weight on the empty side of the scale, balancing the weight of sin on the other side of the scale. When an effort at magical thinking fails, that failure may produce guilt and the guilt may produce depression.

It is very important to note that depression has many causes and guilt is definitely not the only cause of depression. But, one of the causes of depression is guilt! Cain knew his magical thinking had not been productive. And so he produced his own depression. But the abuse cycle does not end with depression. The forces that are unleashed have the potential of furthering the process toward dysfunction.

The fourth stage of the abuse cycle is called "re-creation." Re-creation is the process in adolescence and adulthood in which a person attempts to get magical thinking right by repeating it over and over. It is nothing more than repetitive acts of doing anything which, it is believed, will produce acceptance and gain love. In Genesis 4:6–7, Cain was asked by God to do what was right in order to relieve his depression. God also warned Cain that if he did not do well, sin was "crouching at the door." Cain's conscience scale was out of balance and the imbalance became evident when his brother, Abel, gave a proper offering. In the likeness of his father, Adam, Cain could then blame his brother for without Abel's proper offering,

Cain's improper offering would not have been apparent. However, Cain took the next step. He went beyond what his father had done. Not only did he blame his brother, but he also punished his brother. After all, he said to himself, Abel was the one who made his offering unacceptable. Should he not be punished for his evil act? So, Cain killed Abel. Thus, the act of Adam in blaming his wife had accelerated with Cain not only blaming Abel, but actually killing him as well. The act of re-creation in order to prove his own value or worth continued in Genesis 4:17. Cain built a great city and named it after his son. He was re-creating his act of finding value through his "doing." He was "doing" it again. Only this time, his "doing" was more significant. He wasn't just producing grain. He was building a great city. However, in this case, his act of "doing" insured that the desire to find value on the basis of "doing" was passed on to his son. He named the city after his son Enoch.

But what is the cause of re-creation? Re-creation is repetitive patterns of behavior in the likeness of magical thinking. Simply, it is an attempt to make magical thinking work better than it has in the past. It is an attitude in which a person says to himself or herself, "I don't deserve any better or I didn't get it right the first time; so, I'll try again and again and again."

Re-creation can occur in many ways. Here is an example which is taken from one of the classes we have taught. (The names and circumstances have been changed in order to protect the identity of the individuals.) Jane was the fifth born of eleven children and the oldest daughter within her family. Her father had been a paraplegic from the time of her earliest memory. Her mother was a constant caregiver of her husband and her eleven children. Jane dutifully helped care for her father and her siblings. She found a great deal of recognition because she was so good at being "mommy's little helper." Her magical thinking consisted of "doing" things to help mama. When Jane was eight years old, her mother died due to a tragic accident. Jane became the primary caregiver within the home, caring for both her father and her siblings. Her siblings eventually married and left the home, but Jane stayed on to care for her father. But when Jane reached forty years of age her father died. This presented a crisis for Jane as she could no longer gain acceptance by caring for someone. Then, one day, shortly after her father's death, a door to door salesman came to her house to sell household products. She invited him into her home and immediately fell in love with him. They married almost immediately. Then Jane discovered a secret. Her new husband was a drug addict. She cared for him and attempted to help him with his drug addiction. But she was unable to help him. He died of a drug overdose within three years of their marriage. So, the crisis of having no one to care for again appeared. But Jane had met one of her husband's friends who was also a drug addict. She told her siblings that she was deeply in love again and would soon marry her husband's friend. It was at this point that Jane's sister came to us. She was certain Jane was making a terrible mistake. She had confronted her older sister, telling her how unwise it was to marry another drug addict. But Jane would not listen. Jane was re-creating the act of being a caregiver for her father and her first husband, all in an attempt to re-create the acceptance she had received as a child by being a caregiver. Her sense of value came from caring for sick men. She had become a classic codependent, making certain she always had a sick man to help. She was re-creating her father over and over again.

Another account comes from a man named John. (Once again, the names and circumstances have been changed to protect the identity of the individuals.) John was a missionary who was deeply grieved and, in fact, seriously depressed. He told us that he had just been rejected by a third fiancé whom he had hoped to marry. He asked us why he had been rejected by these three women. Was there any hope he asked? We invited John to join our class and one of our small groups. When we listened to John's story we saw a very sad pattern. He had been abandoned by his father when he was only three years old. His mother then placed him into the care of her older sister, John's aunt. He had only seen his mother every few months, but the memory of her was deeply imbedded into his conscious mind. We began by teaching John how the abuse cycle and re-creation worked. We and the other members of the group then began listening to every facet of his life. He had stated something very interesting in his story. He said he loved his mother's long, beautiful hair. Initially, this indicated nothing unusual. Then, we asked about the relationships he had with the three women whom he had hoped to marry. He kept repeating a very telling statement. As he described each of his potential wives, he successively told us that each of the three women had long, beautiful hair. One of the members of the small group suddenly asked him a question after the statement about long, beautiful hair had been made a fourth time. The member of the small group asked John if there was any similarity between his mother and his three potential wives. Could you be re-creating he asked? John sat and thought for a second. Then, his face suddenly lit up. He said he now knew what was happening. He was trying to find his mother. He had been attempting to re-create his mother in the three women he hoped to marry. Each of these women successively realized he was looking for a mother and not a wife. Each had ended the engagement for the same reason. John had been disregarding their statements concerning his need for a mother, but now he was willing to reconsider what they had been saying. He now knew why he had chosen certain women and why they had fled. He had been attracted to any woman who had long, beautiful hair. He had been reliving a re-creative pattern. The small group began the process of helping John develop a plan to end the re-creative pattern. As the group helped John analyze his situation they even joked that John could only date bald women! But the real plan required that John grow much closer to Jesus. Only Jesus could take the place of the missing parents that had abandoned him. John is now a very happily married missionary. What a joy it was to see this man's life changed.

What is most important about the person who is re-creating is that they are attempting to gain or regain the love they needed from a parent or caregiver. It can be complicated by a what psychologists call imprinting. When a chicken or a duck first hatches out of the shell, the bird will follow whoever it sees for the rest of its life. The one they see may be a human in which case they will actually follow that person, believing the person is their father or mother duck or chicken. This is called imprinting. Imprinting occurs in all animals. And, it also occurs in human children though it takes much longer to complete in human children than it does in animals. Human children can attempt to find or follow the one to whom they have been imprinted for the rest of their lives. Counselors are well aware of this truth. It was also possibly what was occurring in the lives of the two people we just described.

Imprinting has a profound effect in the spiritual realm. If a preschool child, who is raised in a culture where Jesus is worshipped, is asked to describe Jesus, they will invariably describe the man to whom they have been imprinted. In other words, they may describe their father or some other male to whom they have been imprinted wearing characteristic Middle Eastern clothing or hairstyles of Jesus' time. If that child, as an adult, does not maintain a close relationship with the man to whom they have been imprinted, he or she may try to find their fathers by trying to find Jesus, their father image, in some unhealthy ways. They may even try to re-create Jesus in a spiritual leader or the pastor of a church. In this case, the person who is seeking the love of his or her father, in the attempt to recreate, will expect the spiritual authority to behave and even look like the father image they are seeking. If the spiritual authority gives the person enough attention, all may seem well temporarily. But, if in any way that spiritual authority is unable to give enough time to the person who is re-creating, great anger and revenge may be the result. After all, it is believed that the man the person needs is neglecting him or her again, just like when the person was a child. Due to the forces of re-creation, if the father image to whom the person is imprinted was unloving or unkind, the person will seek a spiritual authority who is unloving or unkind. Then, the person will try to win the favor of the authority who is unkind. If the authority is a very kind person and the figure to whom the person is imprinted was unkind, the person will either attempt to make the spiritual authority unkind or they will accuse the authority of being unkind. This is all unconsciously done due to re-creation and imprinting. The effect of imprinting and re-creation can have many bizarre effects within the spiritual realm.

What is the result of re-creation? Repetitive behavioral mistakes can be anticipated. A person may constantly find himself or herself seeking the attention of the wrong person for the wrong reason. Due to the perceived similarity between Jesus and a missing father figure, hc or she may go to a church that has doctrines which match the behavioral characteristics of the person to whom they were imprinted. They may even refuse to become believers because, after all, they couldn't trust their fathers; so, how can they trust Christ? A person may even deny the existence of God as this is a way a person can repay the father who did not care for them the way they needed. They repay him by pretending He doesn't exist. If their father was quite indulgent, the person may go to a liberal church, which has no absolute values, in an attempt to find their missing father. If their father was harsh or cruel, the person may go to a rigid, fundamental church because this is the most likely place to find the missing father.

Regardless of how a person is attempting to re-create and find the love they missed as a child, they will be unsuccessful in the attempt. There is simply no way any human can take the place of a missing father or mother. The love and care of a father or mother has been lost in the person's childhood. The time cannot be recovered. It is lost forever.

The result is the fifth stage of the abuse cycle, greater depression. Re-creation simply does not work. No human being can take the place of a father, a mother, or a primary caregiver. Any attempt to regain the love that was lost as a child is doomed to failure. The result is that the person finds himself or herself facing even deeper guilt than he or she felt as a child when "doing" magical thinking. They have failed again. And, in the same way that guilt produces depression as a product of magical thinking, the same is true of the guilt that comes from failures in the task of re-creation. The only difference is that in this case the guilt and depression tend to be much more intense and can lead to major emotional problems of many kinds. Cain complained in Genesis 4:13 that his punishment was too great. This punishment was not only being excluded from the land of Eden; likely it was also the further experience of depression.

Chapter 5
Real Problems Begin

Problems do not end with re-creation and further depression. The sixth stage of the abuse cycle will follow. This stage is addiction to dysfunctional behavior. This occurs when the person who has been affected by the forces of dysfunction realizes they have not been able to gain the love and acceptance they desperately needed either during the magical thinking phase or the re-creative phase. Addictive behavior is really quite easy to understand. The first time I kissed my wife, I got a great thrill. But, to match that thrill the next time, I had to kiss her a little longer. Then, I had to kiss her twice, etc. Addictions are produced when any behavior partially fulfills, but does not produce complete satisfaction. The behavior then produces a pattern much like a donkey who is chasing a carrot on a stick. We say to ourselves that with just a little more of the fulfilling behavior, we will finally find satisfaction. Unfortunately, the behavior may bring some fulfillment, but it never completely satisfies. It only beckons the person to become more and more involved in the addictive behavior. As an example, when does a person who is addicted to money have enough money? Or, as another example for a local pastor, when is a church large enough to bring fulfillment to a pastor who is attempting to prove himself on the basis of a large following? And unfortunately, with addictions there is always a withdrawal phase. Like a drunk chasing his next drink, there is always a morning "hangover." Pain is always the inevitable result of any addiction. The thrill is only momentary. It is an illusion. But then again, there is always the chance that the next addictive "hit" may be more lasting, more fulfilling. But, it never is!

With addictions, the need for a re-created father or mother intensifies to greater and greater levels. So, those in spiritual authority may find themselves under greater and greater demands from those in their charge. The person who is addicted to re-creating his or her father or mother can become much more controlling and much more critical of those whom he or she is attempting to place into the position of the needed father or mother position. The possibility of significant friction between those in spiritual authority and those who are attempting to re-create the father or mother image through the spiritual authority is significantly elevated. And because addictions only grow with time, with each failure, there is further depression and still more and more attempts to find fulfillment through the same re-creational pattern.

Addictions produce other problems. Because of the process of addiction, the problem worsens with time. There is an ever increasing need to do more and more of what is believed will bring acceptance and satisfaction. Increasing frequency and intensity of eruptions are guaranteed, bringing about constant and growing relationship problems with anyone who might steal the prize of acceptance from the addict. And because addictions do provide a measure of fulfillment, they become behavior patterns which are seemingly inescapable. The addicted behavior patterns are the friend of the addict. They do give a measure of fulfillment. To think of leaving the addiction is very painful to the addict for it means losing the chance to gain satisfaction and acceptance. For this reason, the addict will frequently refuse to cease the addictive behavior. Thus, even if the addiction does not satisfy, it constantly drags the addict into greater and greater levels of addictive behavior. This also means that as the addict ages, the behavior can become more profound for the process has had greater opportunity to control the addict.

In the saga of Genesis, the addictive forces within the line of Cain are clearly evident. In Genesis 4:18–22, we see that men became addicted to all kinds of "doing" including managing livestock, becoming metallurgists, and performing musically. The act of "doing" in order to prove value was growing at an increasing pace due to the addictive process. Thus, these men had become performance addicts.

Surprisingly, addictions are often easy to discover. All one has to do is examine the driving concerns of a person's desires or even his or her prayer life. If a person finds himself or herself praying for success at work, a possible addiction is tied to winning acceptance on the basis of work performance. Nearly any driving prayer focus betrays possible addictions. This also explains why prosperity theology is so popular. It tells addicted people that they can have whatever they believe will give them meaning in life. It tells them they can win recognition and love by following just the right formula. No wonder this theology is so predominant in many Christian circles.

Sadly, when addictions are evident, the seventh stage of the abuse cycle also becomes evident. The seventh stage of the abuse cycle is the progression of pain from one generation to the next. When parents are addicted to some type of performance, their children receive even less love and care than the addicted person received from his or her own parents. The addiction grows with time. Each successive generation is more and more affected by the failure to receive adequate love and care. This generates a continuing cycle from one generation to the next of a growing spiral of pain. Genesis 4 contains a chronology of seven continuing generations of individuals who found themselves trapped in this cycle of dysfunction. The text concludes in Genesis 4:23–24 with the story of one of the most important figures in the line of Adam, a man named Lamech. Lamech was not only the first polygamist in humankind, but he was also a mass murderer. He didn't just scapegoat his wife as had Adam; he demeaned his wife and harmed her by taking two wives. He also bragged that he has killed men in much more frequency and for much less reason than Cain. The point is now made. In the line of Adam and Cain the sins of the fathers continued to follow to each successive generation. With each generation, men become more and more evil. The sins of the fathers had visited themselves on the children (Exodus 20:5; 34:7 & Numbers 14:18). After the events of Genesis 2–4, Genesis 5 describes a line of righteous men through Seth, another son of Adam who was a replacement for Abel. However, the line of righteous men through Seth was destroyed due to intermarriage with those who were not righteous. Eventually, the entire human race was left with but eight righteous individuals, Noah, his sons and their wives. The end of mankind was the result.

There is much more in Scripture to indicate the nature of this problem. Genesis 1–11 is, in reality, a prelude to the saga of the choice of Abraham, the other patriarchs and the nation of Israel. The book of Judges (see 2:10 as an example) explains how successive generations were subject to the forces of growing evil. And the book of Romans is a story of how the problem of repetitive generations of evil has been addressed by God.

At this point, small groups may begin their meetings. The goal for the first day of three to four hours of small group meetings is that as much of exercise1 is completed as possible. The goal is to complete at least questions six or seven of exercise 1.

The Abuse Cycle

1. <u>Love Hunger</u> - Genesis 3

2. <u>Magical Thinking</u> - Genesis 4:1-5

3. <u>depression</u> - Genesis 4:6-7

4. <u>Re-creation</u> - Genesis 4:16-17

5. <u>Depression</u> - Genesis 4:13

6. <u>Addictions</u> - Genesis 4:21-22

7. <u>Love Hunger Passed On</u>
   (with more intensity) - Genesis 4:16-24
   Lamech & Noah's Generation-Judges 2:10ff &
   Matthew 24:37-39

Chapter 6
Addictions and the Complications They Cause

The reality of addictions, formed through the stages of the abuse cycle, produce numerous attempts to find or re-create a missing father or mother in order to complete or find lost nurture and love. Each attempt is an effort to "find my daddy or mommy." This constant re-creation can be directed toward anyone who might possibly fulfill the missing image of a father or a mother. Surprisingly, in cases where there is no male image, either as a father or male caregiver, children have actually been known to try to re-create a missing father image through a sports figure, a superhero, or any suitable alternative. The missing ingredient of love and acceptance from a male figure must be found. A similar problem occurs with someone who is trying to find missing love from a mother.

These patterns of re-creation and addiction, however, develop along very predictable patterns. Whatever seemed to work to gain acceptance as a child will be used over and over again in adulthood. Even if a child was unable to gain acceptance and love, any behavior pattern that was hoped to bring love and acceptance will be repeated. Eventually, a person who is addicted to looking for love and acceptance in a particular way will develop what are called "scripts." A script is a pattern of repetitive behavior which appears over and over again according to learned behavior patterns as a child. A script works the same way as a script in a theatrical play. The actor will always say what is written in the script when the scene of the play reaches a particular point. Scripts can be identified whenever a person finds himself or herself in a stressful situation. Just like an actor, whenever the person finds himself or herself in a particular situation, the behavioral pattern will be repeated according to a predetermined script. As an example, a person who has a problem with rage, may appear gentle and kind. But, when the person is placed in a particularly stressful situation, predictable rage will always result. The script of the person is thus identified through the stressful situation. The rage is a "default" behavior pattern which will always appear when the certain circumstances occur. The rage or default behavior is a scripted pattern of demanding recognition that was learned through the attempts to gain love as a child. Unfortunately, a script never brings satisfaction. Because it is an addictive pattern, it only gives short term fulfillment. But the fulfillment never lasts. It is always followed by the reality of a sense of a lack of satisfaction and the need to participate in more intense and more frequent attempts to find fulfillment through the script.

These scripts can develop according to a particular "role." A role is a nothing more than a distinct type of script which appears over and over again in the attempt to gain acceptance and love. Though there are many different types of roles, therapists have isolated four which are particularly common. The first of these common roles is called the "hero." A hero is a child who always finds a way to make things better by doing something which helps the family or a member of the family. They are the little boys who always do all of the work outside or inside the home in order to help daddy or mommy. They are the little girls who care for siblings or do the cooking or the laundry to gain acceptance and love from mama or daddy. Work and doing things are the primary way that the hero has of gaining recognition. Due to the forces of re-creation and addiction, these people become the heroes of every situation throughout their adult lives. They are the "get it done" folks and often become extreme performance addicts of some kind. They are also those who are always the willing volunteers who seem to be always able to help everyone in some way.

A second of the common roles is called the "scapegoat." The scapegoat always finds himself or herself able to prevent a problem by taking the blame for anything that goes wrong within a family unit. As an example, if father and mother are having a fight, the scapegoat always steps into the situation to take the blame. They say, "Daddy and Mommy, please don't fight; it is all my fault." Father and mother then stop fighting as they realize they are hurting their child. The scapegoat is thus able to prove his or her value by stopping the fight and accepting the blame for the problem. Scapegoats often confess sins that they have not committed. When they confess, they can be enabling others who do wrong as the real wrongdoer is ignored and allowed to continue in dysfunction.

The third of the common roles is the "mascot." A mascot is the little boy or little girl who is always able to stop a family squabble with a joke or a story. When father or mother are fighting, the mascot cracks a joke. Everyone starts laughing and when the laughter is over, the reason for the fight is forgotten. Thus, the mascot saves the family by being a jokester. The value and the acceptance of the mascot are won by being the friendly, always laughing, always smiling fellow or gal who is the life of the party. Mascots are also the children that learned that by smiling they can always gain attention. Thus, the mascot learns to find acceptance by being a people pleaser who always finds a way to deflect problems and gain attention through any winsome way.

The fourth of the common roles is the "lost child." Lost children are the children who were never able to find any way to gain recognition and love. They found themselves unable to help the family whenever any problem erupts. So, whenever stressful situations occurred, they just hid in some way, becoming a part of the furniture so to speak. These are the children who can develop extreme depression as adults for a simple reason. They see no hope. There is no way to solve the problem of finding love and acceptance. They become lost adults as well.

These four roles can bond people together in family units both as children and as adults. In other words, if there was a hero, a scapegoat, a mascot and a lost child in a person's family of origin, they will attempt to find the same actors whenever they congregate as adults. This occurs due to forces of re-creation and addiction.

To explain how these roles bond, I will quote part of my first book, *Toxic Church*. A researcher, named William S. Condon studied groups of people who had never experienced previous interactions with each other. He was attempting to discover why people either liked each other or did not like each other. He put individuals who were unknown to each other into a room and then filmed their interactions. He noticed that individuals organized themselves into preferred groups or circles, rejecting and accepting individuals for unknown reasons. Surprisingly, these preferred groups did not strictly follow demographics like age, gender, race, or socio-economics. He could not determine what it was that caused a person to be acceptable or unacceptable to another individual. Then, by accident, he played the film of the interactions of the larger group in slow motion and noticed something that would change studies of why humans relate to some and not to others. He noticed each member of each particular group moved according to a prescribed pattern similar to every other member of that same group. He also noticed this pattern was distinctive from the movement of every other group within the larger group. Each smaller group had its own distinctive pattern of movement which was only detectable when the film was replayed in slow motion. He also noticed that spoken language choreographed the movements. When he mixed the members of one group with the members of another group, he noticed that they would quickly readjust, configuring themselves according to the similar pattern of movement found among members of their own group. The group members would automatically reject the individuals who possessed a different pattern of movement and automatically accept those who possessed the same pattern of movement as their own. This meant people were accepting and rejecting others not on the basis of any meaningful difference, but only on the basis of an unconscious pattern of movement. He named these patterns of movement the "dance." He discovered that each smaller group had its own distinctive "dance," making possible the unconscious recognition of friend or enemy with acceptance or rejection. He noted that these "dances" were performed by individuals automatically, habitually, and unconsciously. This means that they had no idea what they were doing. They were unconsciously communicating things to others and they didn't know what they were communicating. They were also listening to the "dance" of others and didn't know what they were hearing. Thus, they had no idea what they were communicating to each other. He even noticed that babies adapted to the "dance" of their parents at the age of six months, several months before speaking in identifiable words. They were using the "dance" during the pronunciation of indistinguishable words and sounds.

After further studies, Condon also determined that these "dance" movements were multi-generational, taking two to three generations within a family to change. He thus demonstrated that individuals were unconsciously looking for those who adhered to a "dance" found in their own family of origin. They were literally looking for those similar to their own family members in a totally unconscious, automatic and habitual manner.[1]

What this means is that due to imprinting and the forces associated with imprinting, like the "dance," we all automatically, habitually and unconsciously try to bond with the members of the families we had as children. We will attempt to bond with any whom we might re-create into our childhood family members. When we find ourselves part of any group, including a local church or a ministry team, these forces remain at work. We like or don't like individuals on the basis of factors that have little or nothing to do with any important factor. This is exactly the reason that cliques are born in any group. The problem is that if we had a dysfunctional family as a child, we may unconsciously try to re-create a dysfunctional family as an adult. And we may try to do this in any setting, including a local church or ministry team. So, if our childhood family contained a hero, a scapegoat, a mascot and a lost child, we will attempt to align ourselves with the same characters when we become part of a larger group when we are adults. And once again, we may do this in a local church or ministry team without realizing what we are doing.

These are normal and quite common forces at work in any larger group. And the presence of them does not guarantee conflict or problems. Good leaders are able to find ways to overcome the forces of cliques in any setting. In ministry settings, good pastors, counselors and ministry leaders learn how to train those within their church or ministry how to love each other. In other words, good preaching and teaching can overcome many of these problems.

But, what if . . .

1. (William S. Condon, and Louis W. Sander, "Neonate Movement is Synchronized with Adult Speech," Science (January 1974): 99-101, and W. S. Condon and W. D. Ogsten, "A Segmentation of Behavior," Journal of Psychiatric Research, 5 (1967): 221-25.)

Chapter 7
When Problems Run Amok

Good preaching, teaching and counseling can eliminate much of the problem that comes when individuals within a ministry or church do not get along with each other. But, there are times when reasoning or teaching may have no permanent, healing affect. This occurs when the dysfunction of a person's family of origin reaches such a level that extreme scripting levels have also been reached. In this case, the task of preventing conflict becomes much more difficult. To understand this, we must first examine how these extreme scripting patterns occur.

When a person possesses a great deal of love hunger and has had an extremely dysfunctional upbringing, not only are roles likely, but also intensities of roles. There are five intensities of roles that are commonly acknowledged. These usually develop in tandem with the primary roles we have already explored. One of these intensities is the "placator." A placator is a person who found the only way to maintain harmony within their home of origin was to let the troublemaker win. A placator always attempts to find a way to make everyone happy. And they often attempt to make people happy who are causing major problems. By doing this repeatedly, problem causers are placated. In one of the churches I served as pastor, we had a placator on our senior board. Whenever any difficult decision needed to be made, our friendly placator always insisted that we had to find a "win-win" solution. In other words, everyone had to remain happy. Unfortunately, this often meant that real answers were not considered and troublemakers would be rewarded for their efforts as they were not corrected. The result was that the church was slowly becoming more dysfunctional over time.

Another intensity is called a "rescuer." A rescuer is a person who finds value on the basis of his or her ability to cure the ills of others. A rescuer is a person who is always the one who could negotiate a settlement when any problem occurred in his or her family of origin. When I was a pastor, I recall a professional counselor who I discovered was a rescuer. He asked if I would refer clients to him whenever I found someone who needed his services. And so, I sent quite a few clients to him. But I kept noticing something. When he counseled people, they never reached the time when their counseling was concluded. I knew good counselors usually set a finite number of sessions and then they expect the client either to solve the problem or they discontinue the counseling. But this counselor never discontinued the counseling of any patient that I sent to him. Never! And then I noticed that the clients whom I had referred to him would come to me with complaints that they were not profiting by the counseling sessions. I also noticed that the problems that the clients were taking to him would usually get worse. I saw three couples with troubled marriages divorce after many counseling sessions with him. I actually came to the belief that the way to guarantee a divorce was to send a struggling couple to him for counseling. I soon realized that I couldn't identify anyone who profited by counseling with him. As time went on, I began to understand what was happening as I observed his counseling. He so valued himself as a problem solver for other people that he could not allow them ever to get healthy. If they got healthy, they would no longer need him. And, if they didn't need him, he would lose his reason for being. He would lose his value. So, he actually prevented people from getting healthy by never moving them toward change. He was a rescuer. For a short period of time he served on the senior board of the church. He paralyzed the board with psychobabble about why a problem occurred and why the solutions that were offered would not work. The result was that no problem was ever solved. Problem causers were allowed to continue in dysfunction. The church was getting more and more dysfunctional as he was enabling dysfunctional individuals. I had to find a creative way to remove him from the board. But interestingly, he never stopped pestering me to send clients to him. And he always, always wanted to return to the board. For after all, he said, the board members did not really understand the problems of troubled individuals.

Another intensity of a role is the "victim." Victims are sometimes hard to identify because they seldom complain unless no one notices they are being victimized. In this case, they are apt to tell others they are being victimized by someone. But oftentimes they suffer in silence. They are the children who are the objects of fault finding in their nuclear family. They learn to take abuse as taking abuse seems to calm attackers. Thus, this person actually finds his or her value in being persecuted. Strangely, the only way they received recognition as children was by being blamed for problems. Thus, in adulthood accepting blame and being victimized becomes a pattern of behavior. They must be victimized in order to gain recognition. And so, the victim may accuse others of being abusive when no abuse has been committed. A classic picture of a victim is the wife of an alcoholic. She may be beaten and abused, but she will never leave her husband. And, if the husband should ever become healthy and cease abusing her, she may divorce him only to marry another abusive husband. Why? Because her value comes from others who remark that she is a wonderful woman because she endures the abuse of her husband. If her husband ever stops abusing her, she has lost her recognition. Thus, she either finds ways to make certain he continues to abuse her or she finds another man who will continue to abuse her. This is exactly the problem that organizations like Al-Anon address. Victims enable problem causers because they view themselves as having importance only when they are abused by others. Thus, the problem causers are never corrected. And possibly innocent individuals are accused of abuse.

A fourth intensity is called the "martyr." A martyr is very similar to a victim. However, what the martyr does is seldom secretive. The martyr believes that what he or she does actually saves others from problems in some way. When I was a member of church as a young man, I noticed that every time an altar call was given by the pastor, a man named George would always come forward to confess some horrible crime. He was also careful to praise publicly the pastor for his sermons and tell everyone how his sermons ministered to him deeply. George was a martyr. He believed that by being a public victim, he was encouraging the pastor and helping the church. In fact, the pastor confessed to me that he was weary of George's public statements. He even decided to cease giving altar calls because of George's wearying confessions. George could easily be an enabler of problems. After all, George stated that he was the cause of every problem. And thus, real wrongdoers were allowed to continue to do the things that would cause problems within the church.

Perhaps the most dangerous intensity is that of the "persecutor." Persecutors are not nice people to be around. They grew up in homes where they found value in the act of identifying the sins of others. In dysfunctional homes, this may have been their only way of finding love and acceptance. They were the tattletales who always went to mama to tell her what the other siblings did wrong. The developing persecutor said to mama, "Did you see what he did?" If mama responded in any way positively to the tattletale, the persecutor was being rewarded for his or her behavior. Thus, persecutors become true Adams wherever they congregate. They are always willing to attack the innocent Eves around their lives. Persecutors are very dangerous people because they value themselves only on the basis of ferreting out problems and then correcting those whom they feel need to be corrected. They are the gossips and the critics of many of those within a ministry team or local church. They value themselves so highly for the act of identifying the sins of others that they can even attack the innocent. After all, someone who is wrong must be identified if the persecutor is to find value in himself or herself. There is the potential of attacking someone just for the sake of the persecutor validating himself or herself. And if there is no real wrongdoer, the persecutor says why not invent a wrongdoer? And if there are no problems and no person to attack, the persecutor can actually cause the problems and then identify someone other than himself or herself as the cause of the problem. Thus, they may keep any group tied up in the knots of trying to determine if a problem really exists and who is the real cause of the problem.

Thus, those who have inherited greater dysfunction develop primary roles and intensities of roles. Roles and intensities of roles occur in tandem. So, heroes can become placators, martyrs, rescuers or persecutors. Scapegoats can become placators, victims, rescuers and martyrs. But, they are seldom persecutors for the function of a scapegoat is to accept the blame for problems and not to pass it off to others. Mascots can actually accept any of the intensities. Lost children are somewhat limited as to what intensities they may accept as they cannot be persecutors, rescuers or martyrs. They are excellent victims and placators, however.

There is also the potential that those with intensities of roles can take on varying intensities along with their primary role. Thus, a hero can be a victim at times and a persecutor at other times. Or, a scapegoat can be a both a victim and a martyr. A mascot can be a rescuer and a persecutor at the same time. Any of the intensities has the capacity to affect dysfunctional individuals in various ways.

What is most important to note is that as dysfunction grows through the forces of the abuse cycle; so also do the addictions to roles and intensities of roles. And as these intensities grow, the ability to solve conflict problems through the normal channels of counseling and teaching diminish dramatically. The reason is simple: Those with roles and intensities are also highly scripted. They truly believe their only value in life is to exercise their roles and intensities of roles. If someone attempts to stop them from exercising a role or an intensity of a role, that person is threatening the scripted person's reason for being. The person who attempts to correct a problem can be viewed as an enemy. Thus, any leader, pastor, or layman who attempts to correct a dysfunctional situation can be seen as the enemy who needs to be destroyed. So, even when significant efforts to correct those with these roles and intensities of roles is conducted, the likelihood is that there will only be marginal and temporary change. The person with the dysfunctional role and intensity of a role may feign change in order to dissuade others from seeing him or her as a problem person. But, as soon as opportunity arises, the role and intensity of role will begin to rule the dysfunctional person's life again. The addiction or script is just too strong. And strangely, they truly do believe they are doing the right thing. After all, their behavior pattern is what has always made them important. Their behavior has always worked to correct family dysfunction. How dare anyone ever say that what they are doing is wrong?

How the Abuse Cycle Products Begin to Develop Problem Relationships

Roles

Intensities of Roles

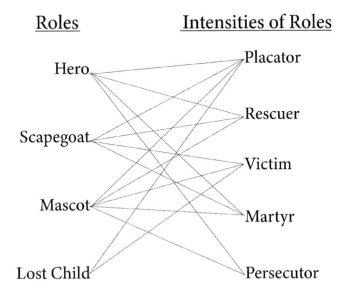

Roles:
Hero
Scapegoat
Mascot
Lost Child

Intensities of Roles:
Placator
Rescuer
Victim
Martyr
Persecutor

Chapter 8
Adam Reappears

What is important to note is how those with primary roles and intensities of roles bond to each other throughout life. In all highly dysfunctional families, persecutors are the primary characters who control the interactions of the family. They are the incarnation of Adam. Persecutors prove themselves by successfully pointing out the deficiencies in others. They will likely become hero-persecutors. The hero-persecutor or HP will constantly attempt to prove himself or herself as valuable by being the hero who identifies the threats to the family and preventing those threats from harming the family. They do this by persecuting those who are identified as threats. Those with other intensities will bond to the HP in the same way they did in their own childhood through imprinting and the "dance." The bonded family is sometimes called a "system." All of the persons with intensities of roles, such as placator, rescuer, victim or martyr, allow persecutors to persecute by placating the persecutor, rescuing the persecutor, or allowing themselves to be victimized or made martyrs by the persecutor. They bond to the HP as it is the primary way they found love as a child and it is seen as the primary way to find love as an adult. Thus, they bond to the HP as placators, rescuers, victims and martyrs through the process of re-creation. The placators and rescuers assist the HP to find victims and then punish the victims for their crimes. The victims and martyrs either offer themselves as victims to be punished by the HP or help the re-created family find and punish others for their supposed crimes. When these scripted individuals join together, they believe they have really found their "home," the place that seems so familiar and so normal. In fact, what they find is not just home; it is a dangerous place where attacks, conflict and victimization are the norm. Everyone has either seen or experienced a home that is filled with conflict. These forces are always at work in these homes. And the tragedy is that these same conflict problems can easily follow the members of the dysfunctional family into their adult relationships. Conflict, persecution and victimization are the norm wherever these dysfunctional people bond.

A problem called codependency can add to the bonding tendencies that exist within those who were reared in highly dysfunctional families. When children grow up in a home with a troubled father or mother, they find a way to hide the shame and problems within the family. To do this they excuse daddy or mommy for whatever problem that exists in the home. As an example, if a parent is an alcoholic and misses a great deal of work, the children will excuse the parent, protesting that the parent is sick rather than admitting the truth. In this way, they come to value themselves on the basis of their ability to prevent shame within a family by hiding a problem. In adulthood, this pattern continues. The adult who was raised in this type of family will attempt to re-create other adults who mirror the problem that was evident in their childhood home. Thus, they find themselves bonding to other troubled individuals. To hide the shame of the group, they hide the problems that exist within the group. They also protect those who cause problems within the group by becoming enablers, taking up the intensity of placator, rescuer, victim or martyr.

There is evidence within the animal realm of the damage that can be done by extreme attempts at re-creation in order to find one's family. When the process of imprinting to a father or mother is in some way prevented from being completed, devastating effects can be the result in the attempt to re-create the lost father or mother. In the 1990s the park authority of the government of South Africa encountered a significant problem. At Krueger National Park, they discovered elephants were killing white rhinoceros with increasing regularity by trampling them to death at a waterhole. This was something which simply did not occur in the wild. So, the question was why was it occurring? Thirty-nine rhinoceros were killed, almost 10% of the rhino population. And, the white rhino population was in danger of extinction. The purpose of the park was to save these endangered animals, not kill them. An answer had to be found. So, the park officials began filming what was happening at the waterhole. It was noted that the problem was occurring with gangs of male adolescent elephants. These gangs had adolescent leaders who would lead the other elephants in attacks which brought about the death of the rhinos. In order to prevent these attacks, the park officials sanctioned the killing of the leaders of these gangs. Five elephants were killed, but the gangs would only recruit a new leader and the attacks on rhinos continued. An examination of the dead elephant leaders brought about an additional discovery. The male gang leaders had over 100% more testosterone in their bodies than normal adolescent elephants. Further tests showed that all of the adolescent male elephants had a problem with raging testosterone. Finally, one of the park workers made a suggestion. There were no large bull elephants in the game reserve. Trucks were not available to bring any large bulls into the park when it was first opened. So, the park officials recruited the help of those who owned large trucks. They brought in some adult bull elephants. The results were staggering! The problem stopped entirely. The gangs of adolescent elephants disbanded. The adolescent males broke up into groups that dutifully followed fully grown, male bull elephants. They began behaving properly. Their testosterone levels also returned to normal. No longer were any rhinos in danger (see CBS News: Sixty Minutes for this story).

What does this lesson teach? The groups of adolescent male elephants that were brought into the game reserve had been subjected to broken imprinting. They had been removed from their fathers. In an attempt to re-create their missing fathers, these elephants formed gangs that were headed by surrogate fathers who were nothing more than bully adolescent elephants who attempted to prove their value by persecuting rhinos. We live in a world with the same problem within humankind. When the imprinting of children is not completed or when they are imprinted to cruel fathers or mothers, the result can be devastating. They can develop roles and intensities of roles which drive them to enable those who would do great evil. This is exactly why human gangs can be a problem.

One of the most frightening realizations is where HPs can be found. They love to go to church! They also love to enter ministry teams! There are simple reasons: A church or ministry team is a great place to re-create a missing father or mother. A pastor is an ideal father image. Thus, a church is a perfect place to either punish a missing father or make a father behave in a way which completes the image of a father that is missing in an HP's life. A church is also a perfect place to become a father to others and thus prove value by re-creating the role of HP that was first used in childhood. In addition, a local church or ministry team is a wonderful place to punish God by attacking a leader or member of the group or church. After all, the HP says to himself or herself, "Why didn't God protect me from my dysfunctional family and the perceived or real abuse I endured? I will punish God for not being there for me." Then, the HP punishes God by selecting a spiritual leader within the church or ministry whom they will attack for the wrongdoing that occurred when the HP was a child.

There are other reasons HPs love to go to church or enter ministry teams. Church is a place where help is supposed to be available to those who are hurting. Since the HP is hurting, church is a wonderful place to seek help. Church is also a wonderful place to volunteer and quickly enter leadership. Churches will never refuse a willing volunteer. So, the HP loves church as it is a likely place to prove one's self and gain love, recognition and eventually a leadership position. Because hurting individuals go to church to seek help, HPs can often find these hurting individuals within a church. These hurting individuals may also allow themselves to be victimized by the HP. Even leaders may be scripted victims who invite attacks. Thus, HPs may be allowed to behave dysfunctionally within many ministry teams. And finally, any church or ministry is a wonderful place for an HP because the HP is addicted to behavior patterns which are meant to win love and acceptance by saving the church or ministry from either real or unreal threats. And, no matter how much attention the HP has won within his or her own family by harming family members or no matter how much attention has been won in the workplace as the HP destroys others at work, there is always the need to continue the addictive pattern. There is always a need for more numerous and more intense addictive eruptions. Thus, a local church or ministry is a certain, eventual target. This means the HP is drawn to a church to harm others like a moth is drawn to a flame. (These are also the reasons mass murderers may often attack a workplace or a local church.)

Not only HPs love to go to church or enter ministry teams. Placators, rescuers, victims, and martyrs love to go to church for very similar reasons. Church is a great place to find a missing or abusive father. So, hurting individuals may seek to find an HP at a church or in a ministry team. Church is supposed to help those who are hurting and, once again, placators, rescuers, victims, and martyrs are hurting people. They love to go to church to get help. Once again, churches are always willing to accept volunteers. So, there is always an opportunity to find a place to belong for these hurting people. And the problem of addictive eruptions also occurs with placators, rescuers, victims and martyrs. So, these individuals will also eventually try to enter a church or a ministry as the need for more numerous and more intense eruptions constantly grows.

What this means is that churches or ministry teams are not necessarily the places to find healthy people. It is sad to say that a church or ministry team may be just as dangerous a place as any workplace or social club. In fact, a church or place of ministry can actually be a very dangerous place. The places which are often considered true refuges from pain and problems may actually become collectors of troubled people who believe they have "found their long-lost home." When people with these types of intensities bond in a local church or ministry, the dysfunctional, re-created family member must complete the re-creative task. They must identify problems as an HP or they must assist an HP by enabling attacks. Conflict, victimization and persecution are certainly part of a church or ministry that contains these types of people. And, this is not an uncommon development. Many churches and ministry teams are known for stress and constant conflict problems.

When these forces are at work at a local church, there is a strong possibility that the church or ministry may not grow. Constant struggles between the members of the church or ministry team may become so engulfing that real, positive ministry will become very difficult and practically impossible. Newcomers are accepted or rejected on the basis of their willingness to allow the dysfunction to continue. Thus, church or ministry team growth is predicated on allowing dysfunction to grow. Strong, effective leaders will find themselves persecuted if they take any action to correct a problem caused by an HP. The entire system, consisting of the HP and all of the enabling intensities within the church or ministry, will protect the HP. The HP, after all, is the one person who makes the church or ministry so much like home. A person who would correct the HP is seen as one who is endangering the homelike atmosphere of the church or ministry. Dysfunctional members may hate their own father or mother. If this happens, this hate may affect the feelings of the members of the church or ministry toward a key leader. In this situation, any leader, pastor, or mature layman is a likely target. For these reasons, the church or ministry leaders become unable to function properly. Plateau, decline and eventual collapse are possible in this circumstance. It is also my contention that the key reason that churches have a natural cycle of growth, plateau and decline is due to these factors. The cycle of decline in churches, which is often portrayed as an unavoidable and natural phenomenon, may be controlled by understanding and addressing these problems. By learning how to correct these problems, the certainty of plateau and decline may be avoided entirely.

There is one other eventuality and this one is quite frightening. A local church or ministry which continues to grow despite the dysfunctional behavior of many of the members may become a cult-like institution. It may have one primary leader who controls all. Everything and everyone are under control of the HP who is either a pastor or a ministry leader. This is exactly the reason a leader like Jim Jones of the People's Temple was allowed to develop a very dangerous cult. It must also be remembered that this happened within the confines of a traditional Christian denomination.

One other frightening reality needs to be considered before leaving the study of the HP and his or her effects. When highly scripted, dysfunctional individuals bond with other highly scripted, dysfunctional individuals, an event called "homeostasis" can occur. The word homeostasis comes from two Greek words. *Homo* means "same." *Stasis* means "static or not changing." Thus, homeostasis means "stays the same." Homeostasis means that dysfunctional individuals within a ministry or church will do anything to maintain the comfortable and dysfunctional home environment they had as children. And that comfortable home environment always included a leader who was an HP. They want a static situation that mirrors the one they experienced as children. This means they will dedicate themselves to maintaining the dysfunctional bonds between troubled people who are harming others within their church or ministry. They will do anything to make certain that an HP remains in control of the ministry. If an HP is removed by circumstances that are beyond the control of those within the ministry, the members of the ministry will take all possible actions to replace the HP. The ministry members will seek to recruit a new HP from outside the ministry. Those within the ministry will even recruit a placator or a rescuer or a victim or a martyr from within the ministry to become the HP. And strangely, the placator or rescuer or victim or martyr will accept the position since they are totally dedicated to maintaining the dysfunctional "home." They will actually deny their own script and become a persecutor if the need arises. And when the new HP is recruited, either from outside the ministry or from within the ministry, the result is the same: Attacks, conflict, victimization, and persecution of others will continue. This is exactly what happened with the elephants. When the group leader was killed, another leader was quickly recruited. This is the reason there are churches and Christian ministries that are repeat offenders, running off successive pastors or leaders and erupting in conflict continually.

And if there is no HP within a church or ministry, there may still be serious dormant problems. For if a highly scripted placator, rescuer, victim, or martyr comes to the church or ministry, they are looking for an HP to complete the task of re-creation of their home environment. All that has to happen is an HP happens to wander into the church or ministry. An instant following of the HP is formed. Trouble ensues. And those who watch it happen ponder how it could happen so quickly.

This has serious ramifications for those who attempt to help a seriously conflicted church or ministry group. If the effort to correct is seen as a threat to the integrity of the dysfunctional family group, the entire group will attack the person or persons who are trying to correct an HP. Even the victims and martyrs will take part in defending the HP. In addition, any positive change on the part of dysfunctional group members is likely feigned. As soon as those who recommended change leave the situation, the dysfunctional group will likely return to the behavior patterns which caused the conflict. Problems will begin anew.

And something else must be understood. When a positive leader is attacked in this type of situation, the result may be disastrous because he or she may develop an extremely defensive posture. Deviant behavior in the form of anger or depression or both on the part of the leader is possible. When this occurs, the members of the dysfunctional family group within the church or ministry will gladly point out the deviant behavior of the leader. The result is predictable. The days that the positive leader has within the ministry are numbered. This is exactly the reason many pastors resign or are forced to resign from local churches or ministries. And though not as public, this is the reason positive leaders leave ministries or local churches for false or unknown reasons.

Re-created Dysfunctional Family Seeking a "Hit"-Rivals Expected to be Victimized by all

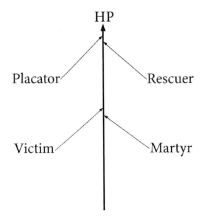

Rival Other Leaders
(or anyone deemed fit for destruction by the HP)

Chapter 9
A Problem That Needs a Solution

When a person is scripted to a dysfunctional role and an intensity of a role, the problem will likely remain hidden. First, the script of the dysfunctional person is seen as normal, natural and spiritual by the troubled individual. The way the person has found of compensating for feelings of inadequacy has seemingly always worked. To abandon that method seems self-destructive. There is no reason for doing so. Thus, the definition of normal, spiritual behavior is controlled by the dysfunctional script. The person relates to Scripture with strict adherence to some passages and blatant disregard for others. The persecutor holds rigorously to Luke 17:3, "Be on your guard! If your brother sins, rebuke him!" Other passages may go completely unnoticed. In like manner, the placator holds to Matthew 5:9, "Blessed are the Peacemakers." The victim holds to Philippians 1:29, "To you it has been granted to suffer." In this way, each script is steadfastly maintained. Any suggested change is resisted since it is seen as un-Scriptural. And besides, the scripted person tells himself or herself, "Other behavior patterns just don't work; I'd rather do what comes naturally. And after all, what comes naturally is also Scriptural."

Other problems are evident when a person is scripted to a dysfunctional role and an intensity of a role. The person can easily fail to define his or her own script. After all, the behavior pattern seems normal and natural. It is the way the scripted person has always behaved. Therefore, it isn't a script; it is the way people ought to behave. For the same reason, the more profound the script, the less likely a person is to consider lessons that would change the scripted behavior. Once again, it is not viewed as a script; it is viewed as normal and correct behavior. And, the more profound the script, the more likely it is for the scripted person to see a person who confronts the behavior pattern as an enemy. A person who confronts those with serious scripts can even be seen as a person who does not respect Scripture for they fail to note the self-justifying Biblical confirmations of scripted behavior. For this reason, a person with a dysfunctional script may regard the words of this book as mere "psychobabble." And, even if the scripted person should ever seemingly change, there is a strong likelihood that the person will return to the addicted behavior pattern for, once again, it is seen as normal, natural and Scriptural. Conflict resolution will have limited effect for when pushed, the scripted person will only feign change during a time in which the person's actions are under examination. When the examination ceases, the addicted person will return to comfortable behavior patterns which have become a part of the scripted person's character.

There are other frightening consequences of an addiction to a dysfunctional script. A person may be utterly unaware of the fact that they are hurting others. A persecutor does not see himself or herself as a persecutor. They see themselves as heroes who are protecting an entire ministry organization from a person who they deem dysfunctional. This is why Jesus said, "Father forgive them; they don't know what they are doing." They really didn't know what they were doing. They thought they were saving their nation (hero) by killing Jesus (persecutor). And one more thing: Since this behavior is addictive, it will only grow worse. The power of addiction means the need for eruptions will grow more numerous and intense with time.

These factors provide for a conclusion which must not be avoided. Mollifying a person who is addicted to harmful scripts is an exercise in futility. In fact, mollifying a dysfunctional, scripted person is enabling that person for it allows that person to continue destructive behavior patterns. An addicted person will only grow worse in the performance of dysfunctional scripts if they are not stopped. And a person who will not stop destructive behavior patterns in others may be an addicted placator or rescuer who justifies himself or herself in actions which fail to stop evil and lead to further and continuing problems of conflict, victimization and persecution.

Unfortunately, the depth of these problems is often overlooked by those who are empowered to address conflicted ministries.

These are the same forces that have wreaked havoc in American families, causing divorce and family dissolution for several generations. Due to the forces of addiction, these forces are now spreading to wherever people congregate, including local churches and ministries. The result is that church and ministry conflict and resulting dissolutions continues at an ever-increasing rate. There are Biblical answers, but if the true causes of conflicted churches and ministries are not understood and accepted, these solutions may not be applied. The truth is there is only one real answer. It is to apply the Biblical injunctions which are either misunderstood, misapplied or unintentionally disregarded. It is time to turn our attention to the Bible for answers which cure and prevent toxicity in church and ministry organizations. There is an answer. We begin with "The Antidote," the central focus of this book.

This is usually the time in which small groups may meet for their second session of three or four hours. The goal during this session is to complete exercise 1, all ten questions and to complete questions one and two of exercise 2.

Part 2
The Antidote

"If you do well, will not your countenance be lifted up? And if you do not do well, sin is crouching at the door; and its desire is for you, but you must master it." Genesis 4:7

Chapter 10
Turning Point

In 2006 I was a mess. I had been experiencing extreme abuse from key church members during several of the years I had served as a senior pastor. I felt I could no longer function in a local church. Even though I had just received a call from a promising congregation, I was too emotionally distraught to consider another pastorate. All of the churches we served had grown, some quite dramatically. We had seen many conversions and baptisms in our pastorates. But even though we had seen considerable success, I found I was unable to prevent criticism and personal attacks from the occasional antagonist that I had encountered. I was unable to master any techniques which would overcome the pain that seemed to accompany a significant part of our pastoral ministry. The Lord graciously offered a call for us to serve a seminary in Singapore. The church we planted in Toronto, many years earlier, included many Singaporeans. When we arrived in Singapore, we discovered many of our old friends from Toronto waiting to greet us. It was a true joy. But I was left with the nagging question: What was it that I had done wrong which had produced turmoil during portions of my pastoral ministry? What could I have done to prevent the periodic personal attacks from a few key individuals within the churches I served?

As I began teaching at the seminary, one of the courses I taught was Old Testament survey. As I prepared for this course, I began to see something very interesting in the story of Cain in Genesis 4. God had offered Cain a critical decision in Genesis 4:7. God had told Cain that if he did well, his countenance would be lifted up. He also told him that if he did not do well, sin was crouching at the door. The question that came to me was what did "doing well" include? I realized that Cain was the first man who had to deal with the sins of his father. His father, Adam was the only man who had no harmful heritage with which to deal. I realized that Cain's decision was no different than my decision or the decisions of any man who has had to deal with the sins of father Adam.

As I pondered Cain's situation, I realized that Cain was dealing with a critical problem which also faced his brother Abel. They both knew they were naked (Genesis 3:7). They both saw themselves as unacceptable and unworthy of receiving the love and approval that all men need due to the sin of Adam. This problem was so intense that something had to be done to overcome the difficulty. Genesis 4 tells us that Cain and Abel dealt with the problem in very different ways. Abel offered an animal sacrifice, a picture of the coming sacrifice of Jesus. Cain offered the product of his hands. In making the offer of an animal sacrifice, Abel had declared that there was nothing he could do. God would have to make Abel acceptable in the coming sacrifice of Christ. Abel's offering was truly an offering of faith. He was trusting in God to provide the answer for his problem. Cain, on the other hand, declared his own ability to deal with the problem. His offering was exactly the opposite of Abel's. Cain was declaring that he could make himself acceptable through his own efforts. Thus, Cain's offering was not an offering of faith. It was unacceptable to God.

But to understand the true nature of what each of these men did, it is critical to realize what they were trying to accomplish. If they were to become acceptable, the question is from whom would they attempt to gain acceptability? Abel declared, through his sacrifice, that he would only deal with the task of being acceptable to God. He would not concern himself with being acceptable to men. Cain, on the other hand, was looking for acceptability from men. His dependence on himself and his own labor demonstrated that he had no need for God or God's help. He would find acceptability on the basis of what he himself could accomplish. And this acceptability would be that which he could receive from men. The true nature of what it meant for Cain to "do well" was based on whether he would seek acceptability from men or from God. This is the critical question which each of us face in the task of "doing well." Will we seek the acceptance of men or God? In Genesis 3:8–12, we see this was exactly the same question which God had presented to Adam when he failed to answer the three questions properly. God was giving Adam the opportunity to depend upon God and ask for forgiveness. Adam chose to depend on his own efforts by making excuses and blaming God and Eve. By doing this, he chose to seek the acceptance of someone other than God. This has been and always will be the key to understanding how it is that we reverse the problem presented by Adam and Cain and "do well" as Abel had done. Each of us has to decide whether we will seek the approval of men or the approval of God (John 12:43 and Matthew 22:37–40).

But we must also realize what happens when we seek the approval of men rather than God. When we need the approval of men, we also place ourselves in the position of being controlled by those same men. If men choose not to give approval, they have the power to prevent us from experiencing any real joy in this life. We find ourselves always tyrannized by the question as to whether men will give us acceptability. A nagging fear concerning approval from others prevents us from having any real contentment in this life. In addition, if I depend on the approval of men, others may become my rivals. Any acceptability that others gain may threaten my own sense of acceptability. I may see the acceptability of others as a possible detraction from my own acceptability. I may find myself unable to give others acceptability because of the fear that the popularity and approval of others may threaten my own popularity and approval. Thus, any chance for real fellowship is highly unlikely. In addition, I can't be a strong leader as I may fear the possibility that others will not follow me and thus I may lose acceptability. I may constantly find myself fearing whether or not I am acceptable as a leader in the eyes of those around me.

As I contemplated the necessity of "doing well," I came to a simple conclusion. The issue for me in my failures in pastoral ministry had nothing to do with how I could change others and prevent the attacks which became so troubling. In fact, I realized I have no power to change others. But I do have power to change myself. If I can "do well" and stop seeking or needing the approval and acceptance of men, those who seek to harm me have no power over me. Simply stated: They can't hurt me if I don't care what they do to hurt me! The real secret for a pastor who is under attack is not to try to change others; the secret is to change himself! Each of us must learn how to "do well" and stop seeking the approval of men.

But one more question concerns me. What is it that prevents me from escaping the tyranny of needing the acceptance and approval of men? There is something inside of me that really hurts when others attempt to harm me or disrespect me in some way. I really believe the powers of magical thinking, re-creation, and addiction have taken their toll on the inner man within me. But I also believe that we all are hardwired for failure in this way. This world and the powers of the Fall have dealt us a problem that we cannot overcome alone. We see ourselves as unacceptable. There is a little voice, crying out within each one of us that asks, "Is there anyone out there who will love me? Is there any way I can get you to notice me?" What is the answer? How can we stop seeking or needing the acceptability of men? Understanding the steps that are a part of The Antidote provides solutions for this problem.

Chapter 11
Step One of *The Antidote*: Adam's Mistake

What can we do to end the problem that Adam began? How can we reverse the problems caused by the Fall and apply the principle of "doing well" from Genesis 4:7 to our lives? The first step lies in understanding the mistake that Adam made. Perhaps, by understanding a little more about what Adam did, it just may be possible for us to understand what steps are necessary to reverse the process and prevent much of the pain that comes into each Christian's life as a result of Adam's sin and the accompanying abuse cycle. After Adam and Eve had eaten the forbidden fruit, as described in Genesis 3:8–12, they hid themselves from God. When God asked Adam where he was, he excused himself by telling God he was afraid because he was naked. What did Adam fear? Why was he afraid that God would see him naked? Then, God asked him two other questions. The first was who told you that you were naked? The second was, "**Have you eaten from the tree of which I commanded you not to eat?**" Recall, God certainly knew the answer to all three of these questions. In this passage Adam excused himself by blaming both Eve and God. In other words, Adam didn't answer the last question that God posed with a simple "**yes.**" "**Yes**" was the answer that God was offering to Adam. But, Adam failed to do one very important thing: He didn't confess with a "**yes.**" Rather, he scapegoated both Eve and God. God was giving Adam an opportunity to confess with a simple question. But Adam failed to confess. And why did he fail to confess? Why did he hide himself from God? The loss that Adam feared was a simple one: He feared that his nakedness would make him unacceptable in the eyes of God. He also feared confession. For admitting sin might also make him unacceptable. So, he hid from God. He refused to confess. And, he blamed Eve and God.

65

These verses teach us one simple truth. The problem Adam had was a fear that he might not be acceptable. And, unfortunately, each one of us has inherited this fear from Adam. This need plagues us, producing almost every relational problem we face. The need to find acceptance causes us to value ourselves on the basis of performance. It is also the cause of our tendency to underrate the value of others. Each dysfunctional script is formed into a person's character as the result of this need. Hero-persecutors and their enablers all behave the way they do because they have a deep need for love and acceptance. So, the reversal of what Adam did is a simple answer for the problem. To reverse what Adam did, all Christians have to do is find a way to understand how acceptability can be found and maintained without the use of scapegoating others and denying sins. So, addressing the need to gain acceptance is critical if the problems associated with human conflict are to be addressed.

How do we, as Christians, find and maintain our sense of acceptability? First, we must do what Adam did not do. We must learn to confess. This answer is clearly given in 1 John 1:9, "If we confess our sins, He is faithful and righteous to forgive us our sins and to cleanse us from all unrighteousness." If we are forgiven and cleansed from all unrighteousness, we are acceptable! There it is! Adam failed to confess. And to reverse the damage that Adam did, the first step for you and me is to learn how to confess. All we have to do is just to say "yes" about our sins. Doing the opposite of what Adam did is part of the process of finding and maintaining acceptability. In the same manner as Adam, Cain attempted to manufacture his own means of winning acceptability. The only difference is that he didn't initially scapegoat Abel as Adam did with Eve and God. Rather, he refused to depend upon God in the task of finding acceptability. Later, when he discovered that his attempt to win favor on the basis of his own efforts failed, he scapegoated his brother. Sin was crouching at the door as the Lord said. So, he didn't just scapegoat Abel; he also killed him. After all, Abel's good offering made Cain's bad offering look bad. Did not Abel deserve punishment? Abel's sacrifice was the opposite. It was a confession that he could do nothing to gain acceptability. The way we become Christians is by the confession of our sins and inviting Jesus to come into our hearts (Revelation 3:20). Paul told us in Colossians 2:6 that as we have received the Lord we should also walk with Him. This means a day to day process of confession is the key to "doing well" as Abel had also "done well." But what is included with confession? How does confession affect us and how do we learn to confess? Proper confession is the first part of The Antidote.

Chapter 12
Step Two: Understanding Confession

Confession is frequently misunderstood. True confession allows a Christian to experience the grace and love of God. Scripture teaches that humility is the path to receiving God's grace. This is demonstrated in James 4:6 and 1 Peter 5:5 where we are told that God gives grace to the humble. The word "grace" in these verses is an important one. In Greek, it is the word *charis. Charis* can be translated into the English word "grace," but it can also be translated into the English word "gift." In fact, the English word charismatic, which refers to a Christian who uses God's gifts, is derived from the Greek word *charis.* So, God gives grace to the humble, but He also gives a gift. When we humble ourselves by confessing our sins, we receive God's grace or gift.

But what is this gift that is imparted through confession? How does confession as an act of humility bring us a gift of grace like that promised in James 4:6? The promise of 1 John 1:9 is that when we confess, we are forgiven and cleansed from unrighteousness. The problem is: There are times when we don't feel forgiven after we have confessed. There are times when we don't feel cleansed from unrighteousness. There are times when we don't believe 1 John 1:9. In fact, there are times when we focus only on our human condition, our nakedness and our unacceptability. In other words, there are times when no matter how much we confess, we still don't feel acceptable.

There is a reason this occurs. Many Christians don't understand the simplicity of confession and the effect it can have on each individual life. The truth is many Christians really don't understand what confession is. They think that confession means we must beg God for forgiveness. They also believe that if a Christian happens to fail to confess a sin, he or she will not be forgiven for that unconfessed sin. Some Christians mistakenly believe that confession is the means to gain forgiveness. Some Christians even believe that if they happen to fail to confess a sin, when they die, they risk being condemned to hell for that unconfessed sin!

This understanding of confession is wrong. In fact, the concept of confession may be one of the most misunderstood truths in all of Scripture. The Greek word for "confess" in 1 John 1:9 is the word *omologeo*. It is derived from two Greek words: *omo* which means "same" in English and *logeo* which means "word" in English. From the word *omo* the English word homosexual is derived. It simply means "same sex." From the word *logeo,* or *logos* in its form as a noun, we have the derivative for the English word, "word." It is found in John 1:1 where we read, "In the beginning was the 'Word' and the 'Word' was with God and the 'Word' was God." Thus, we see a fitting translation for *omologeo* in Greek, or "confession" in English is: "same word." We have another way of saying "same word" in English. We can also use the English word "agree." Thus, to confess is simply "to agree." So, how do we agree with God in the task of confession? God says two things about sin in the life of the believer. First, He says it is sin. Second, He says it is forgiven. So, to agree with God means that we confess we have sinned **and** we confess that our sin is forgiven! Scripture says that we are not forgiven because we confess. We are forgiven because of the blood of Jesus. Confession is not only confessing that a sin was committed; it is also confessing that the sin is forgiven!

But what does forgive mean? In Hebrews 10:17, we see God says, "Their sins and lawless deeds I will remember no more." This is very difficult for Christians or for that matter, anyone to accept. The reason is simple: God forgets; we don't! We have a real problem forgetting our own sins because we already see ourselves as unacceptable due to the effects of the sin of Adam in our lives. Don't forget: We all see ourselves as naked. We look at ourselves through the biased prism of guilt. Therefore, we readily entertain the idea that any sin makes us more unacceptable. For this reason, we can't forget! But, God does! Forgetting our sins is the gift that God gives to the humble! Recognize the depth of this gift. If I go to God in prayer with a statement about any sin, past, present or future, Hebrews 10:17 tells us that God literally says, "What sin? I can't remember any sin! You didn't do any sin. I have no idea what you are talking about!"

Colossians 1:21–22 puts it very well. It states, "And although you were formerly alienated and hostile in mind, engaged in evil deeds, yet He has now reconciled you in His fleshly body through death, in order to present you before Him **holy and blameless and beyond reproach.**" (emphasis mine). Isn't that a wonderful gift! We are holy and blameless and beyond reproach; not because of anything we have done, but because of what He did for us through His death. But there is a problem. We don't always feel holy and blameless and beyond reproach. Once again, confession is the answer. This is the gift of God which is evidenced as the result of our humility. In confession, we are not only confessing our sin; we are also confessing the fact that our sin is forgiven **and forgotten!**

Colossians 2:13–14 further states, "And when you were dead in your transgressions and the uncircumcision of your flesh, He made you alive together with Him, having forgiven us all our transgressions, having cancelled out the 'certificate of debt' consisting of decrees against us and which was hostile to us; and He has taken it out of the way, having nailed it to the cross." The concept of a "certificate of debt" as it is used in this verse is important. Every Roman magistrate kept record on the pages of a scroll about the good and bad things that a citizen would do. If a citizen had done a crime requiring punishment, the page recording the crime would be torn out of the scroll and given to those who would punish the criminal. It would be placed above the criminal's head if he were to be crucified. It was called the "certificate of debt!" Colossians 2:13–14 is telling us something quite dramatic. When Jesus died on the cross, the sign above His head didn't just say He was the King of the Jews. What it really said was Jesus was being punished for our sins. If we have accepted His gift by putting our faith in Him, our certificate of debt was placed above His head! When God looks in His scroll for our sins, He can't find anything there. Not a single word about what we have done wrong remains. Why? Because it was torn out of the scroll and nailed above the head of Jesus. Our sins have not only been forgiven; they have been forgotten!

What about the sins we have not yet committed? The book of Hebrews plainly indicates in chapter 10 that if His sacrifice did not cover all of our sins, past, present and future, He would have to come back to earth and die again. This chapter teaches us that His sacrifice is permanent, covering all of our sins. Hebrews 10:10–14 tells us, "By this will we have been sanctified through the offering of the body of Jesus Christ once for all. . . . For by one offering He has perfected for all time those who are sanctified." Hebrew 7:25 further tells us, "Hence also He is able to save forever those who draw near to God through Him, since He always lives to make intercession for them." So, all of our sins, past, present and future are forgiven and forgotten! This is the gift of God which He gives to us. The act of confession is the act of confessing that we are forgiven for our sins **and** confessing that our sins are also forgotten!

The problem is that we constantly persecute ourselves about our past sins and the sins we commit every day. We don't forget our own sins. But Jesus says I have forgiven and forgotten. When we confess, it is not the act of begging God for forgiveness because He has already forgiven us. Remember: We aren't forgiven because we confess; we are forgiven because of the blood of Jesus! Confession is the act of agreeing with God that we are forgiven through His blood! And it is the act of agreeing with God that our sins are forgotten through His blood! In fact, an important part of confession is the act of asking God to forgive us for remembering our own sins! And even that part of confession contains this truth: We must not only confess the fact that He forgives us for remembering our own sins; we must also confess the fact that He has forgotten that we have ever remembered our own sins! This is the gift of God that comes from the humble act of confession: Living forgiven lives! This is what allows us to truly live the Christian life; a forgiven life that is free from guilt, shame or any need to gain acceptance.

Confession can best be explained by a story about a little boy and his father. Let us say that a little boy and his father are very close—so close the father will do anything to maintain his fellowship with his son. After a week of work for the father and school for the little boy, the father and the little boy plan a fishing trip on Friday night and Saturday. They plan to drive to a lake, spend the night, and have a great day of fishing. All week long the little boy sees his father preparing the equipment for the fishing trip. On Friday afternoon, after school, the little boy is invited to his friend's house for a time of play. The little boy accepts the invitation. However, the play continues too long. The little boy has lost track of the time. He realizes his father is waiting for him to come home so that they can leave on the fishing trip. Now he has a problem. He is afraid his father will be very disappointed in him and he is afraid to face his father. He is afraid he may not be acceptable in his father's eyes. The little boy's friend invites him to stay for dinner. And because the little boy is afraid to face his father, he agrees. Then, even more afraid to face his father, he finds an excuse to stay longer at his friend's house. Finally, it is late at night. The little boy now knows his father is likely very upset. The little boy now must decide how he will return home. When he arrives at his home, he hopes that everyone is asleep. He carefully opens the door so as to not make any noise. His hope is that he can crawl into bed, unnoticed. The little boy, however, has a father who loves him and wants constant fellowship with him. So, the father, wide awake and very concerned about what has happened to his son, waits until late at night, anticipating the return of his son. He is not waiting to punish his son. He is waiting because he loves him; he is concerned about his welfare. Where could he be (Genesis 3:9)? But the little boy does not know he will not be punished. So, the father gives the little boy a wonderful way to live forgiven. It is called confession. All the little boy has to do is come into the house and say, "Father I have arrived; I am late; I have sinned; AND father, I know I am forgiven and my sin is forgotten." The father holds his arms out to hold his son. He says, "Yes son you are forgiven and I can't remember what you did. All I want to do is hold you. I want you to know that I love you. Now come to my arms. Allow me to hold you and love you!" The little boy runs to his father's arms, sits on his lap, and experiences the love his father has for him.

This is the way the act of confession works. It is bestowed on those who are humble enough to confess. The gift is constant fellowship with Him. In other words, God has given us a psychological trick, if you will allow me to describe it that way. The trick is that we are given this marvelous step of accepting and admitting that we are forgiven and our sins are forgotten. This is the gift of God that comes from our humility, expressed through confession.

How could this have been applied in Adam's situation? Adam simply needed to say "yes" when asked if he had eaten the forbidden fruit. All he had to do was to say I have sinned by eating the forbidden fruit. All he had to say is I confess the sin of doubting that I am acceptable. All he had to say is I confess the sin of hiding myself from the Lord. All he had to say is I confess the sin of thinking I am unacceptable. I confess the sin of not making certain Eve was protected from my failure. And finally, all he had to say is I confess the sin of remembering my own sin! If Adam had confessed, the entire account of Genesis would have been entirely different (1 John 1:9 and Malachi 3:6). Cain made the same mistake as had his father, Adam. He was offered an opportunity to "do well," but he chose not to confess. Rather, he chose to add to his sin by killing Abel.

The same offer that was made to Cain is offered to you and me through the step of humbling ourselves through confession. When we confess, we don't ask for forgiveness. In fact, if we find ourselves asking for forgiveness, we must ask God to forgive us for the sin of asking for forgiveness. To ask for forgiveness is a denial of what Jesus has already done for us on the cross. Confession is confessing that we are forgiven by the blood of Jesus. And, confession is the act of confessing the fact that our sins are forgiven and forgotten. A daily routine of prayer which includes confessing that our sins are forgiven and forgotten is the pivotal, first step in gaining a sense of our own acceptability. I frequently find that those who take our seminary course struggle with this concept. I am often asked, "But don't we have to confess in order to be forgiven?" I then share this simple statement: "We aren't forgiven because we confess; we are forgiven because Jesus died for us on the cross. Please examine Colossians 1:21–22; 2:13–14; Titus 3:5, etc. etc. etc.

Chapter 13
Step Three: Learning What to Confess

The first part of The Antidote is confession. Understanding how proper confession is done can be quite freeing for Christians who either do not regularly confess or confess improperly by begging for forgiveness. But, the second part of understanding confession can be even more freeing. Our confession must not only include our sins; it must also include the motives and root causes of our sins. The reason: The cause of our sin is likely based on an attempt to gain acceptability from men in some way. The attempt to gain acceptability was what motivated Adam to hide from God, scapegoat Eve and fail to confess. The attempt to gain acceptability was what motivated Cain to grow angry when his sacrifice was not received favorably by God. If Christians are to reverse the sin of Adam and Cain in their own lives, any attempt at complete confession must also include admitting or confessing that the root causes of our sins are sins. If we don't confess the sin of holding to the root causes of our sins, there may be a continuing temptation to commit the sin again. Why? Because the cause of the sin, the desire to gain human acceptance, has not been forsaken. The root cause will likely produce further sins whenever we sense a need to gain the acceptance of men. When we are able to confess the sin of holding to the root causes of our sins, we gain significant freedom from the tyranny of having to gain the acceptability of men.

A Biblical perspective on seeking to gain the acceptance of men is important. The act of placing emphasis on human acceptance risks placing greater emphasis on the acceptance of men than on the acceptance of Jesus (John 12:43; 1 Thessalonians 2:4; Matthew 22:37; etc. etc. etc.). When we seek human acceptance, we fail to understand several simple truths. We have all the acceptance we will ever need from Jesus. We don't need anymore! We cannot lose his acceptance as it was given to us when we put our faith in Him. And, we cannot gain any further acceptance from Jesus because He gave us all the acceptance that He has to give. Simply stated: We have no need for further acceptance for His acceptance makes us complete in every way. Looking for human acceptance is a disregard of God's acceptance. It is looking to men rather than to God. It is, therefore, idolatry as it places something, the acceptance of men, in the place of God. In addition, seeking our own acceptance in the eyes of other humans is nothing more than a veiled attempt to glorify ourselves. This too is idolatry for it is an attempt to set a primary goal of glorifying ourselves rather than glorifying God. Ancient people worshipped idols to gain fertility or wealth or power. The idolatry was done in order to procure the things which the ancients believed would bring importance and the all-consuming prize of acceptance from men. In the same way that the ancients resorted to idolatry to get the gods to do something to give the pagan a sense of importance, Christians may resort to idolatry of a more sophisticated nature. Christians may also idolize the act of seeking the acceptance of men. This is the basis for all our scripting problems which lead to conflict and pain of every sort. Every script is formed into our character in order to gain acceptance. Regardless of any justification for seeking the acceptance of men, idolatry is still idolatry. It is a sin. Remember these verses:

> You shall have no other gods before Me. You shall not make for yourself an idol, or any likeness of what is in heaven above or on the earth beneath or in the water under the earth. You shall not worship them or serve them; for I; the Lord your God, am a jealous God, visiting the iniquity of the fathers on the children, on the third and the fourth generations of those who hate Me, but showing lovingkindness to thousands, to those who love Me and keep My commandments. (Exodus 20:3–6).

Some examples of why confessing the root causes of a sin as being a sin is important. If a boy is playing football for his high school football team and he happens to scream obscenities at a referee who gives an unfavorable call during a game, the confession of the boy should involve confession to the Lord for the act of screaming obscenities. The boy should also ask the referee and all who heard the obscenities for forgiveness as well. But, proper confession, which is part of The Antidote, requires that the boy go to the next step. His confession must include admitting the reason or the motivation which caused him to sin is also a sin. In this case, a likely cause is that the boy was attempting to gain the acceptance of men on the basis of a win on the football field. Not only must the boy confess the sin of speaking profanity; he must also confess the sin of trying to gain the acceptance of men on the basis of athletic performance. If he does not confess the root cause of the sin, a repeat of the sin is likely because the boy has not admitted the true cause of his sin. He may find himself offended the next time a referee's call does not go his way because he is still attempting to find value on the basis of his own athletic prowess. Thus, he may repeat the sin. And, very importantly, his confession should also include the sin of his failure to be content in the love and acceptance of Jesus.

As another example, imagine a woman verbally criticizes another woman because she always dresses in a manner which makes her look very beautiful. The sin is critical language. Anything she has said in criticism must be confessed as a sin. But, confession according to The Antidote requires that she not only confess the sin of a sharp tongue; she must also confess the sin that caused her to verbally criticize the other woman. In this case, the possible cause is that the woman is attempting to gain her own value and sense of acceptance from men on the basis of her own looks. Therefore, she sees the other woman as a rival who must be criticized. She must not only confess the sin of criticizing the other woman; she must confess the sin of trying to gain acceptance from men on the basis of her own looks. Otherwise, she may find herself criticizing some beautiful woman again. And she must confess the sin of not being content in the love and acceptance of the Lord.

Another example requires a little deeper analysis. A man speaks to his wife unkindly, telling her she is getting a bit too heavy. Or he rebukes her because she doesn't cut her hair the way he likes. The sin that must be confessed is the sin of unkind words. But The Antidote requires that he must also confess the sin of holding to the root cause of his caustic remarks. In this case, one of the possibilities is that the man is critical because he wants to gain the acceptance of others on the basis of his wife's beauty. He may want a "trophy wife." Thus, he must confess the sin of trying to gain the acceptance of men on the basis of his wife's looks. Otherwise, he may find himself criticizing his wife again. The man must also confess the sin of not being content in the love and acceptance of the Lord.

Another example that requires deeper analysis occurs when a woman is constantly critical of her daughter-in-law. Once again, confession according to The Antidote requires not only confession of the sin of the ways she rejects her daughter-in-law; it must also include the confession of the sin of the reason for the rejection. In this case, it is possible that the mother-in-law is attempting to win the acceptance of men by ruling her family. Thus, the sin that must be confessed is the sin of trying to win acceptance from men on the basis of her ability to dominate others. Or, her motive may be rooted in the failure of her own marriage. Perhaps she is trying to gain more attention from her son by criticizing his wife. The motive may be to gain more attention from her son in order to compensate for the loss of love she has from her own husband. So, the sin that must be confessed is trying to gain the attention of her son in order to compensate for the lost love and acceptance from her husband. If she doesn't confess this sin, she may find herself criticizing her daughter-in-law again. Her confession must also include the sin of her failure to be content in the acceptance and love of the Lord.

And finally, let us consider a pastor who verbally criticizes another pastor who has a larger church. The Antidote requires that he not only confess the unkind words, but he must also confess the sin of holding to the cause or the root of the unkind words. In this case, a likely culprit is his desire to win acceptance from men on the basis of the size of his church. So, confession must include confessing the sin of trying to win the acceptance of men on the basis of the size of his ministry. Once again, if he fails to confess this sin, he may find himself criticizing other pastors again. And his confession must include the sin of his failure to be content in the acceptance of Jesus.

In each of these cases, there is a possible problem. How is the root cause of the surface sin issue accurately discerned and confessed? Sometimes, root causes of sin are relatively easy to discover. But, there are other times when the root causes of sin are not so easily discovered. Steps to help in the task of understanding why a person does what he or she does are needed. Oftentimes, the help of a professional Christian counselor is helpful. But somewhat surprisingly, the task of uncovering the root causes of sins can often be accomplished through the intervention of a caring group of Christian brothers or sisters. The small group meetings and exercises that are suggested in the appendix of this book are designed to help accomplish this purpose.

Chapter 14
Step Four: Understanding the Addiction Problem

Recognizing what sin issues should be confessed, including the root causes of those sins, is quite important in applying the first part of The Antidote. But there is a major impediment to recognizing what the root causes of our sins may be. This impediment is addiction to various scripted behavior patterns. Behavioral addicts regularly try to win the prize of human acceptance. But recall how addictions are formed. Any addiction never completely satisfies, but it does provide partial fulfillment. Thus, it beckons a person to continue to participate in the addiction in the hope that true satisfaction can be found. It never is. The addict only continues, interminably, to chase the prize. Forsaking the addiction becomes something to be feared for to forsake the addiction risks losing the prize of acceptance. Thus, addictive scripts, meant to bring human acceptance, hold an addict tenaciously within the grasp of various behavior patterns. And never forget that addictive scripts sometimes produce a painful "hangover." After the temporary thrill that comes from partial fulfillment, the addict may feel guilt for the act of harming others in the act of trying to win human acceptance. But because the person is addicted to the behavior patterns that produce this pain, he finds himself hopelessly trapped in the process of producing his own pain and the pain of others. In addition, the addict enjoys the temporary result of finding a partial measure of human acceptance. To cease performing a behavioral addiction that brings a measure of fulfillment seems unwise and even foolish. To do so means that the person loses the hope that any real fulfillment can be found. Thus, performance addictions can become the Christian's secret friends for they provide help in the task of finding acceptance. In fact, due to the forces of the abuse cycle, attempting to gain the favor of others can become so much a part of a person's personality that these efforts seem to be quite natural. They are seen as behavior patterns that should be recognized by all men as normal and healthy behavior. Sadly, rather than confess the sin of seeking the acceptance of men, the addict may resort to denial and scapegoating. In this case, it is almost impossible to escape the addiction. The addict will consistently resist any efforts to bring about the confession of the addictive root causes of sin as being sins. In this case, the only cure, other than the discipline of the Lord (Hebrews 12:5–6), is for loving Christians to confront the addict when he or she harms others (more about confrontation will be discussed in later chapters).

Consider this example: A Christian woman who prays for her children's success may unconsciously pray for her children because of the recognition she might receive from others if her children succeed in some area of life. When this happens, a problem arises. When are a woman's children good enough to give her complete acceptance? They will never be able to meet her need for acceptance because her addiction to proving her value on the basis of her children's success can never bring complete satisfaction. She can only gain partial fulfillment. Thus, every success of her children only beckons her to push her children for more and more success. There is no end to her desire to push her children. Thus, a woman, even a Christian woman, can become what is known in Asia as a "Tiger Mom," a woman who pushes her children unmercifully. She is a hero who saves her children by pushing (persecuting) them. She is an addicted HP. She will find it very difficult to stop pushing her children. She will likely find herself unable to confess the sin of attempting to find her fulfillment in her children's success. To do so risks losing the acceptance of others when her children succeed in some way. (This is one of the reasons depression rates for primary school children in Singapore is quite high).

In like manner, a Christian businessman may pray for success in business because a successful business will give the businessman a greater sense of acceptance and recognition. The problem is: When is a businessman successful enough to gain all the acceptance he needs? A business is never big enough or successful enough to accomplish all that a businessman needs to gain complete satisfaction. He can only gain partial fulfillment through his business successes. Due to the forces of addiction, his efforts will eventually drive him to manipulate and use others in the task of winning the prize of more money and a bigger business. The inevitable result is that the businessman becomes a tyrant who constantly controls and harms others to gain greater and greater levels of success. In reality, this businessman is nothing more than a true performance addict. He saves his business (hero) by pushing his employees and attacking his competitors (persecutor). He is an addicted HP. He also will be very resistant to ceasing the effort to build a bigger business. He will find it difficult to confess the sin of holding to the sin of trying to gain his acceptance on the basis of business success. To do so risks losing any acceptance he might receive as a result of his business accomplishments.

The same problem can occur within the life of those in Christian ministry. (In fact, in my experience, this is extremely common.) The biggest difference is that in Christian ministry, the addict can deceive himself or herself by believing that the addiction isn't an addiction; it is part of God's will for his or her life. A pastor can drive himself to bring more and more people to his congregation. With more people, more and more are being won to faith. The pastor may have a simple goal to win people to faith. However, it is possible that his real goal is winning the acceptability of men by having a larger congregation. Thus, any gimmick or program that promises more church members becomes extremely important in the pastor's eyes. Any person who prevents the winning of others to the church by opposing some program or gimmick becomes an enemy. A staff member who does not produce results is seen as a problem because he is not helping the pastor achieve the prize of numbers. And any pastor who has a bigger church becomes a target of criticism as the pastor of the bigger church has become a person who can potentially steal the notoriety of the pastor of the smaller church. Thus, the pastor saves the world by building a bigger church (hero) by pushing his staff and church members to perform while attacking other pastors and other churches (persecutor). He is an addicted HP. He will find it very difficult to ever admit that the act of attempting to find value on the basis of a large church is a sin. To do so risks the loss of acceptance that comes from building a bigger church.

A similar addiction problem can occur within the life of a church staff member or missionary on a mission team. If a staff member or missionary is addicted to winning the acceptance of men, the implementation of a suggested program by a pastor or mission leader might become a problem if the program is unpopular among some of the members of the ministry or church. Not only might the staff member and the leader be at odds, but also the entire organization may collapse into conflict as sides are chosen, one favoring the pastor or leader and the other favoring the staff member or team missionary. In this case, the missionary or staff member may also be an addicted HP who saves the church or ministry (hero) by fighting the pastor or leader and dividing the church or ministry (persecutor). Once again, admitting the true nature of the root cause of the sin is unlikely. To do so risks losing the acceptance of church or ministry team members.

I remember a missionary school director who told me his goal was to have the finest missionary training center in Asia. Why? What difference would this make to the mission director? Would he be more important? Would God love him more? This man demonstrated extremely driven behavior. He would do anything to make his school the best and his graduates the best missionaries (hero). The secret culprit was an addiction to gaining the acceptance of men. The end result was an ineffective training school which drove the missionaries unmercifully. Missionaries in his charge were being harmed through his numerous attempts to make his school the "best" (persecutor). The missionaries in his charge weren't being loved; they were being used! They were used in the sense that the purpose of the director was not to better prepare the missionaries; his purpose was to glorify himself through the performance of the missionaries. He was an addicted HP. And, it is, once again, unlikely that he will admit the sin of trying to find value on the basis gaining the acceptance of men. To do so risks the loss of the acceptance he might gain from having an extremely efficient missionary training school.

I also remember the leader of a mission group who railed at one of her older staff members when she complained about the pace of a forced walk on a cobblestone street. As my wife and I observed, the pace was much more like a run than a walk. The leader refused to slow down for her staff member. The leader simply said, "We must stay on schedule if we are to see lost souls come to Christ (hero)." These platitudes sound so spiritual. But, if the real goal is to prove value on the basis of making others perform according to rigid requirements, the opportunities for rivalries, conflict and harming others appear (persecutor). In this case, the staff member was lamed by the forced pace and unable to walk throughout the remainder of the two-week conference. She required surgery to correct the damage that was done to her knee. The leader, sadly, will never find the satisfaction which Jesus intends by these means. Her acceptance does not require a fast-paced walk on cobblestone streets. Jesus only requires that we walk with Him, while showing love and kindness toward others (Micah 6:8). The mission group leader is an addicted HP. She will likely never be willing to admit the root cause of her sin, the desire to find acceptance in the eyes of men. To do so would risk losing the prize of the praise of men.

A classic example of men who were addicted to proving their value on the basis of gaining the acceptance of men is found throughout the gospel accounts. The religious leaders of Israel had invented a system of theology and religious rules and regulations which they believed brought value to themselves. In fact, they were addicted to the pattern of proving their value on the basis of their teachings. When Jesus confronted their errors by breaking their Sabbath laws and teaching a different theology, they began to plan a way to kill Him (John 5:18; 12:43). So addicted were they to their methods of gaining acceptance that they were willing to commit murder rather than to forsake their mistaken addictions. They could not leave their systems of theology and rules for to do so would be forfeiting what they believed was the ability to gain value in the eyes of men. They were addicted HPs who were saving the nation (hero) by killing Jesus (persecutor). The likelihood of their willingness to confess the root cause of their sin, the attempt to gain the acceptance of men, was quite low.

The root cause of these types of efforts is always the same: A Christian may be trying to gain the acceptance of others because he or she isn't living in the knowledge that Jesus is the only source of acceptance that a Christian ever needs. The real problem with performance addictions, however, is how they affect a Christian's ability to apply the first part of The Antidote. Because of addictive forces, **the addict doesn't want to stop being an addict!** There is an intense resistance to change of any kind. The result is that the addict cannot confess the root causes of a sinful performance addiction. The grace of God, evident in living forgiven lives, is never realized.

I remember a man who went through the exercises that are contained in the appendix of this book with me. He spoke of extreme abuse in childhood. As a little boy he was abandoned by his mother and savagely brutalized by his father. However, he also insisted, tenaciously, that the extreme abuse of his childhood had not affected him. He told each member of his small group that he had nothing to confess (1 John 1:8, 10). He steadfastly insisted that every motive of his life was meant to please Jesus. He stated that he would never do anything with a motive of winning the acceptance of men. He was also the principal leader of the primary decision-making board of his church. Sadly, this man later was the cause of a major split within his church. Even though he insisted that he did not need the favor of men, he had to prove his value in the eyes of men by maintaining himself in a high position of leadership (hero). He did so by attacking others who wanted a rival to take his leadership position (persecutor). He was a performance addict who maintained human acceptance by leading the church and saving it from any supposed threat. He was a true hero-persecutor who had the opportunity to stop harming others, but he chose to go the way of Adam, Cain and Lamech. He did incredible harm in attacking some of the members of his church. He also was so addicted to being an HP that he would not confess the sin of trying to gain the acceptance of men by being the primary leader of the church.

I also remember when a denominational leader took our course. Members of this man's small group pointed out to him that he appeared to be addicted to winning the favor of men through his ministry. He bitterly rejected the observations of these other men within his small group, even though the observations came from other ministry leaders. He demonstrated extreme opposition to our course and has steadfastly done whatever he can to discredit the course. Why does he do this? Addiction! He is addicted to winning the favor of men through his ministry and fears ceasing his addictive activities for in so doing he would lose the opportunity to win the acceptance of men!

Thus, a major impediment to confession is an addiction to any act of "doing" in order to gain the acceptance of men. Addictions to "doing" can become so controlling that the addict may find himself or herself completely oblivious to the sin issues of his or her own life. Deep down inside, an addicted person does not want to confess the sin of "doing." To confess means the addict will lose the acceptance that is partially received through the addiction. The root causes of sin and the actual sins themselves continue, unconfessed. The final result is that the addict is opposed to anyone who might unveil the true root causes of sin issues that control the addict's life. And, the addict dislikes the type of material that this book presents as it forces consideration of issues that the addict does not want to consider.

Chapter 15
Step Five: Overcoming the Addiction Problem

Proper confession includes a willingness to forsake addictions to activities which are believed will bring about human acceptance. But addictions are very controlling. This leads to a question: How is the impediment of performance addiction to be removed in the application of proper confession? Because many of us are scripted to behave according to performance addictions, leaving these methods of gaining human acceptance may be quite difficult.

There are several answers. Something which should never be overlooked is the power of the Holy Spirit to convict men regarding sin (John 16:7–8). People really do change as the result of the conviction of the Holy Spirit. And some can change as the result of their own personal Bible study or due to the teaching of a gifted Bible teacher. Some are teachable because they are wise enough to know they don't have all of the answers of life. And some even change when they read books like this book or some other book which confronts these problems. Some profit by Biblical counseling in which the root causes of problems in the life of the performance addict are explored. However, one of the greatest teachers is human experience. When a person experiences pain, one of the beneficial results is teachability. When a person knows that what they have been attempting in life has been unsuccessful, they begin to explore new possibilities.

There is also a method which my wife and I have found very helpful. This method is small group meetings of teachable, committed brothers and sisters in Christ. We look for those who are open to exploring the nature of their own pain either because they are wise enough to know they don't have all of the answers of life or because the hard knocks of life have convinced them that they need to find new answers for the problems they face. Regardless of the reason, we have found that when teachable individuals enter into one of our training seminars, dramatic, positive change is the result. The appendix of this book includes four exercises which we have been honing with additions and deletions for over thirty years. These exercises are designed to help uncover the root causes of addictive sin issues in a Christian's life. With the help of a group of teachable, committed brothers or sisters, any tendency to deny or excuse an addictive sin issue can be lovingly confronted (Galatians 6:2). With the help of the confidentiality statement within the appendix, signed by each participant, we have found these exercises provide significant help for a person who is struggling with sin issues and the addictive motivations which drive those issues. The result is the possibility of Christian living, complete with forgiven, fulfilling and joyous Christian lives.

I often cannot share how these exercises have been a help to others because most of the stories are confidential. But, I can give you a personal example of what I learned as the result of my own self-examination through the exercises contained within the appendix of this book. With the help of these exercises and a small group that helped me through these exercises, I learned a great deal about myself.

I was raised in a home with a loving father who was also a workaholic. I loved my father and desperately wanted more time with him. I learned that to gain time with my father, I had to work with him. He was a building contractor and there was plenty of work to do with him. I became very good at work on the construction site. My efforts to win my father's love worked! My father and I became very close as I worked quite regularly with him. I also had a sibling who did not have the same need I had and did not see the value of doing a great deal of work. This sibling constantly found ways to avoid any work around the house. Unjustly, I was always victimized in some rather creative ways as I was frequently manipulated by my sibling to do his work. Whenever I complained to my mother, I discovered that the result was that I would be unfairly punished because I was causing a "fuss." This injustice taught me to keep my mouth closed and put up with my sibling and his manipulative ways. But, I always resented my sibling because of his actions.

How do these things affect me as an adult? As an adult, I am addicted to work. I constantly struggle with overworking. Unconsciously, I am working to gain acceptance, the same acceptance I received from my father. I have difficulty accepting the fact that Jesus loves me even if I don't work hard. Thus, I am a highly scripted hero. I have always worked very, very hard in ministry. I can also be a hero-placator as I learned early in life not to complain. Complaining to my mother never worked. In fact, it didn't win acceptability; it destroyed it. So, as an adult, I constantly refuse to confront. I am a placator. I fear losing acceptability. This means that I often allow troublemakers to escape correction. I am totally capable of enabling problem causers wherever I serve. I can also be a hero-persecutor. Whenever I am around people who don't like to work, I find myself very resentful. I have no doubt that these people can sense my resentment. This means I can be a hero-persecutor when I am around people whom I perceive to be lazy. Now, how did I learn these things about myself? It wasn't through my own reflection though that was certainly a part of the process. Many of these insights came from others who were willing to sit with me in an examination of my experiences and family patterns. These caring small group members helped me to be aware of where my default scripts lie and what matters should be subject to confession. (See Proverbs 11:14; 12:15)

The results of this help from caring brothers have led me to these realizations. Here is what I need to confess: First, I need to regularly confess the sin of trying to gain the acceptance of men. I need to regularly, daily confess the sin of trying to gain acceptance through work. I need to carefully manage my work, being certain that boundaries exist in which I limit the amount of work I do. Second, I need to confess the sin of withholding proper, loving, Biblical confrontation. Confrontation must not be withheld from those in my charge who fail to be faithful in their work or participate in any other sinful activity. If I withhold confrontation, I am demonstrating the script of hero-placator. If I fail to confront those who are unfaithful, the problem of becoming a hero-persecutor is possible as I may resent the person who needs correction. So, this confession is very important. As I confess these things, I acknowledge that I am already forgiven and the sin is forgotten. And, very importantly, as I repent, I ask Jesus to forgive me for valuing myself on the basis of being a hero, and I ask Him to help me understand that the acceptance He gave to me on the cross is all that I need. Finally, I purpose daily to refuse to seek the acceptance of men and live in the freedom that I am totally acceptable to Jesus no matter how much work I do or don't do.

The solution for the addiction problem is a simple one. If the Lord does not provide correction for the Christian who is attempting to win the approval of men, loving Christian brothers or sisters who are willing to confront the brother or sister is the best solution. However, proper Biblical confrontation is not possible if the person who confronts is concerned about his or her own personal acceptance from the person who should be confronted. In other words, confrontation is best accomplished by the person who loves the person who should be confronted so much that they disregard their own need for acceptance. This is accomplished when the confronter has applied proper confession about the need to gain human acceptance to his or her own life first. More about confrontation is presented in a later section of this book.

Chapter 16
Step Six: Repentance

Proper Biblical confession is the first major part of The Antidote. Once proper confession has been applied to a Christian's life, the second major part of the The Antidote can be applied to his or her life. The second part of The Antidote is simple, Biblical repentance. The Biblical, Greek word for repentance is *metaneo*. *Metaneo* simply means "changed mind" in English. So, to repent, one must simply change his or her mind. One must learn to think in new ways. But how does one change his or her mind and think in new ways when addicted to a scripted behavior pattern? If our sin is seeking the acceptance of men, the simple step of repentance is to change our minds by ceasing attempts to gain the acceptance of men, and, instead purpose to seek and apply the acceptance of Jesus. In other words, the second step of repentance in applying The Antidote is simple. The second step requires a purposeful determination to bathe one's self in the love and acceptance of Jesus rather than to seek the acceptance of men.

The first way to begin the process of changing one's mind, living in the love of Jesus, and repenting is through prayer. A prayer of confession needs to be so much a part of a Christian's being that every time the slightest twinge of an attempt to gain the acceptance of men appears, it is quickly subdued. Here is an example of the confession and repentance that any Christian can and should use in a prayer. It is simple prayer which should be part of the Christian's daily or even hourly prayer regiment.

> Lord I have sinned. I have been trying to gain the acceptance of men by doing (heroing, placating, rescuing, martyring, witnessing, preaching, teaching, befriending, counseling, vision

casting, piano playing, handicrafts, sports, etc.-you get the idea, whatever "doing" that we use to gain the attention of others). Thank you for forgiving me and for forgetting this sin. I purpose to live without regard for human recognition, knowing that I already have all the recognition I will ever need from you. I accept that I cannot lose your acceptance even if I fail at everything. I repent of my desire to gain human acceptance as I already have your love and acceptance. I ask you to give me the power to stop looking for any human recognition or acceptance. I ask you to help me focus only on the acceptance which you have already given to me. I purpose to live only for You, seeking only You! In His name, I pray. Amen!

Included in this regiment of prayer is regular Bible study and a commitment to memorize Scripture. When a Christian has developed a healthy, regular devotional life, closeness with Jesus is realized. This leads to an ability to forsake the need to gain the acceptance of men. Without this closeness with Jesus, the likelihood of avoiding the need to gain the acceptance of men is quite difficult.

Prayer and a healthy devotional life are a good first step in repenting and ending the tyranny of performance addictions in a person's life. However, addictions to scripted patterns of behavior require a great deal of discipline to overcome the damage that they may do. These addictions, by their nature, can reappear at any time. They are our default behavior patterns. So, changing our addicted default behavior patterns requires tenacious efforts. Another, additional way to address the problem of constantly reappearing addictions is through the use of the Stop-Think card. (See appendix 1 of *Toxic Church*).

Here is how the stop-think card works. The first step is to come to an understanding of why and how seeking the approval of men has become a priority and maybe an addiction in your life (John 12:43; 1 Thessalonians 2:4). Then, determine what Scripture verses address how and why seeking the approval of men in this particular way is wrong. Memorize these verses. Next, take a 3x5 index card and write on one side of the card, in large bold letters, the words "STOP-

THINK." On the back of the card, write the following four steps (in very small letters).

1. Seeking the approval of men by . . . is a sin. Cite your memorized verses. Repeat them from memory.
2. Confess the sin of seeking the approval of men by . . . cite and repeat from memory 1 John 1:9. (Remember: Confession means you are forgiven and the sin is forgotten.)
3. State your purpose to repent and ask for God's help in the process. Cite and repeat from memory Exodus 20:3 & 1 Peter 5:8
4. Repeat steps 1, 2, and 3 ad infinitum ad nauseum

The purpose of the stop-think card is simple. By repeating Scripture and purposing to repent of a particular sin, the mind is slowly changed. Changing the mind is what repentance is. Thus, repentance is slowly completed. The stop-think card should always be carried so it can be used at any time. In addition, the stop-think card should be used daily, during one's devotions or whenever these circumstances are experienced:

1. when with others who don't recognize your presence or your accomplishments
2. when with others who criticize you, either justly or unjustly
3. when with others who get too much attention and recognition
4. when with others who abuse or manipulate you
5. when with others who refuse to do what you ask them to do
6. when experiencing the feeling of shame
7. when experiencing a lack of peace

In addition to a carefully designed devotional life and the stop-think card, an individualized plan is needed to complete the process of eliminating harmful addictive scripts from a person's life. A plan which each Christian can use to eliminate these addicted behavior patterns is contained in exercise four of the appendix. Exercise four consists of a ten-step program which has been consistently used by professional counselors with great success in changing the harmful, addictive behavior patterns of a person's life. Thus, through prayer and a healthy devotional life, the stop-think card and an individualized plan, each Christian can repent and live in the freedom that Jesus has given to each one of us, the freedom that comes from living in the truth that we are completely acceptable in Him and no other acceptance is needed. In this way, we can fully live in the knowledge and reality of Jesus' love for us! But never forget that in order for these steps to provide true benefit, confession of the sins involving the ways we have been programed to seek the acceptance of men through the powers of the Fall must be included. And, in this application of confession and repentance, The Antidote becomes a part of our lives!

Chapter 17
Victory In Jesus

The benefit of applying The Antidote to the Christian's life addresses many of the needs of life. To understand the benefits of The Antidote, realize what happens when a Christian confesses the sin of trying to gain the acceptance of men? The freedom that is gained through proper confession allows a person to ignore seeking the love of men and provides the opportunity for him or her to live only in the love of Jesus. For the Christian this is a simple, but important truth: Acceptance comes from Jesus. It cannot be lost. He gives it to the Christian unconditionally. The Christian can't gain more acceptance from Him because He has given the Christian all the acceptance there is to give. And, there is nothing that can take away the Christian's acceptance as Jesus will never stop accepting each Christian. Acceptance from men is an illusion. It can never satisfy. Why? Because the nature of addiction means satisfaction based on the acceptance of men can never be realized. Addictions only provide temporary and incomplete fulfillment. This means there is no contentment in this life if it is based on gaining the acceptance of men. However, true contentment can be found in Jesus. Basing contentment on the love and acceptance of Jesus is the one, true way human contentment can be found. This means the addictive process of trying to find fulfillment from the acceptance of men no longer tyrannizes the Christian.

The acceptance found in Jesus means Christians don't have to "do" anything. No longer is guilt for not "doing" something a part of the Christian life. No longer does the Christian experience a tension which requires him or her to "do" or not "do" something to gain acceptance. This freedom from having to "do" something in order to gain acceptance provides an opportunity to experience great joy.

And this is all made real to each Christian by the determination to confess the sin of trying to gain the acceptance of men and instead to bathe in the acceptance which only Jesus offers.

Because Christians no longer have to "do" anything to prove value, the potential to develop harmful, addictive scripts in an attempt to win value from others also ceases. This means the potential to hurt others through harmful scripts is controlled. No longer do Christians have to resort to being an antagonist or the enabler of an antagonist in order to win acceptability. And since there is no longer the experience of guilt due to the behavior associated with harmful scripts, Christians also avoid much of the pain that comes from the guilt associated with the exercise of these scripts.

In addition, because Christians who have applied The Antidote to their lives don't have to find ways to gain the acceptance of others, they no longer find themselves bitter when others fail to praise them for any particular "doing." They can accept and love others, even when the others fail to note how very important their own "doing" is. After all, in confession Christians are admitting they don't need the acceptance of others because they have all the acceptance they need in Jesus. Thus, others lose an important power. They can't control individual Christians by their giving or failing to give acceptance. The Christian doesn't need the acceptance of others as Jesus' acceptance is complete.

Christians also don't have to fear others as potential competitors for their acceptance when others "do" more than they themselves "do." The "doing" of others is no longer a threat. Christians who have applied The Antidote to their lives don't need to compete with anyone for acceptance because they have realized that they already have all the acceptance they will ever need! This means they are free to praise and love those who "do" well in whatever activity they might perform. Jealousy becomes a factor which no longer affects. They can then love others who are able to "do" things in a very special way. This allows true fellowship to develop, a fellowship without jealousy and one which rejoices in other's accomplishments.

And, as is important in many "shame based" cultural contexts, a person who confesses the sin of trying to win the favor of men doesn't have to be concerned with the shame that might occur due to any human failure. In fact, shame has no power as living in the knowledge of the complete acceptance of Jesus means a Christian simply can't be shamed. Jesus' acceptance overrules any shame a Christian might experience. Therefore, an absence of acceptance from others means nothing! Shame has no effect. If a Christian senses shame, he or she merely confesses the sin of trying to gain the acceptance of others by trying to avoid shame. Shame is no longer possible. What freedom (particularly for those who live in a shame-based culture)!

The Antidote provides other remarkable results. If a Christian never purposes to seek human acceptance, he or she has the freedom not to become a highly scripted hero. Heroes need and seek acceptance through acts of "doing." But, if a Christian has forsaken attempts at gaining human acceptance through acts of "doing," being a hero is no longer necessary.

Enablers, like rescuers and placators, also develop new freedom. Enablers enable because they want the acceptance of the person they are enabling. But if a person doesn't need human acceptance, he or she also doesn't need the acceptance of those who offer acceptance on the basis of being an enabler. This means the Christian doesn't have to remain silent when others are being harmed by an HP. He or she also doesn't have to stand by when they themselves are being treated badly by an HP. Why? Because they no longer fear losing an HP's acceptance or the acceptance of others in the HP's system. Simply put, they don't have to be enablers any longer.

Victims and martyrs, who are also enablers, have the power to confront when they are being unjustly attacked. They don't have to enable dysfunctional behavior on the part of hero persecutors and their enablers by allowing themselves to be victimized. And, maybe more important, victims and martyrs have the power to leave dysfunctional ministries when they are being attacked. This also provides a great deal of relief for those who have found themselves being persecuted.

Recently, I shared a dinner with a close personal friend who has retired after being a denominational leader for many years. During our conversation, this friend made a curious observation. He said that he had found that success in ministry was coupled with an "I don't care" attitude. He didn't mean that those in ministry should not care for or love others. What he meant was that those in ministry should not be concerned with whether others give or do not give acceptance. I totally agree with my friend. However, I would add that this quality is not only valuable for those in ministry. It is valuable for every Christian! This "I don't care" attitude can only be gained when we live in the knowledge that all the acceptance we will ever need comes from Jesus.

Tied closely to the "I don't care" attitude is the benefit of The Antidote for those who wish to develop leadership skills. In fact, it may not be too strong a statement to say that The Antidote may be one of the most important Biblical principles for leadership that exists. Here's why: The greatest impediment to leadership is the fear that one's leadership is not accepted by intended followers. But, if one doesn't care about whether or not the follower follows, great freedom can be demonstrated. The leader can lead without concern for rejection. A leader is never intimidated by the fear that no one will follow. The leader just leads and is free to leave the results in the hands of the Lord. The leader develops what often described as a leadership personality: a self-defined person with a non-anxious presence.

Perhaps the greatest personal benefit of The Antidote is peace. Matthew 6:26–27 says, "Look at the birds of the air, that they do not sow, neither do they reap, nor gather into barns; and yet your heavenly Father feeds them. Are you not worth much more than they? And which of you by being anxious can add a single cubit to his life span?" Zechariah 4:6 adds, "Not by might, nor by power, but by My Spirit says the Lord of Hosts." How is living by these precepts possible? The answer is very simple: Live without concern for the acceptance of men. Attempts to prove one's self in the eyes of men is what pushes Christians to perform in ways in which they are attempting to produce more than the providence of the Lord allows. There is only one real goal in our lives as Christians: Christians are responsible to be faithful and to abide in Jesus—nothing more! It is not the Christian's job to produce results (1 Corinthians 3:6–9). In fact, Christians are not in control of results; they are only in control of effort. This effort consists of faithfulness in work and abiding in Jesus. It is abiding in Jesus that produces results, not our own efforts

(John 15). This is dramatically freeing. This means each Christian can stop driving himself or herself unmercifully when results are limited. The Christian can simply do his duty as a faithful and abiding Christian and leave the results in the hands of God. Results are not the goal! Faithfulness and abiding in Jesus is the goal! This is perhaps one of the greatest benefits of The Antidote. Christians are free from the worry and drudgery of needing to produce.

Christians can also behave in a manner that benefits others through the application of The Antidote. The Christian no longer has to prove his or her value by bragging about accomplishments. Others no longer need to be belittled for their absence of accomplishments. In fact, no pecking order on the basis of those who are seen with or without accomplishments is necessary or even tolerated. Each Christian is free to love other Christians without regard for accomplishments or the absence of them.

Christians who live according to The Antidote also cease the need to dominate or control others. The task of coercing others to assist in the task of "doing" something to prove the value of the addicted person is no longer necessary. Those in the charge of a Christian, in work or ministry, no longer become potential threats if they fail to assist in the task of winning acceptance through performance. In addition, those in the charge of the former performance addict can't control the former addict by doing or not doing what is asked. Why: Because not doing what is asked no longer threatens a loss of acceptance.

There are other benefits from The Antidote. When men are looking for acceptance from men, it is possible that their prayers may be contrary to the will of God. The person may be praying for something which will win the acceptance of men. The Lord knows that to answer this type of prayer may enable an addiction. So, prayers, though they may ask for good things, may be contrary to the will of God. If God answers that type of a prayer positively, He may be actually hurting a Christian (James 4:2b–3) for He is enabling the Christian's addiction. But when the need for human acceptance is forsaken, prayers take a dramatically different direction. Christians stop praying for the things that will give them acceptance. They begin to pray for things that will truly be a benefit to others, to themselves, and to the Kingdom of God. They begin to pray according to the will of God (1 John 5:14–15). Their prayers become much more effective. Prayer life dramatically changes and fellowship with the Lord improves as well.

The Antidote provides another benefit. The experiences of each Christian's life, orchestrated by the God who loves that Christian, are under His control (1 Thessalonians 5:18). There are times when the events of each Christian's life are very puzzling. The Christian may ask himself or herself what the Lord is doing in his or her life when things simply don't happen the way it is hoped. When a Christian understands that God is thwarting attempts to gain human recognition and empowering the Christian to live in His acceptance, the Christian's perspective on the events of his or her life takes a remarkably different direction. The Christian begins to understand many of the ways of God in a much deeper way. The Christian can begin to understand why Scripture tells us to thank God for everything as everything is the will of God (again see 1 Thessalonians 5:18). Failed hopes and dreams may often become understandable. Much of the pain of life is thus overcome. Fretting about not having the things previously thought necessary and focusing on the only thing we do need, a closer walk with Jesus and His people, becomes a part of life.

Another benefit of The Antidote is an understanding of 1 Corinthians 10:13. This passage teaches that whenever the Christian is under some trial, God will provide a way of escape so that he or she can endure. When a Christian understands why God prevents success in attempts to gain human acceptance, the Christian also begins to understand the way of escape from many trials. The purpose of God in allowing trials is often to remove the Christian from the need to gain human acceptance. His purpose is to teach the Christian patiently to delight in Him and His acceptance. The way He does this is often by allowing Christians to face circumstances in which attempts to gain the acceptance of men fail (Romans 8:28–30). In this case, the way of escape is simple: Comply with the will of God and cease activities which are performed in an attempt to gain human recognition and acceptance.

There is another, somewhat surprising, benefit of The Antidote. Some theological systems tell Christians that they can have anything they want if they just find ways to believe God will answer their prayers favorably. However, the things Christians want may be related to the attempts that are made to gain the acceptance of men. In that case, it is unlikely that God will always answer prayers the way they are desired. To answer these prayers may enable addictions which harm Christians and those around them. When Christians understand the bounds of their prayers (again see James 4:2c–3), they can then understand the limits of those who propose this theology. They can then also understand the potentially erroneous systems of theology which promise that Christians can have anything they ask through what is called believing prayer. In fact, what is sometimes called believing prayer may be, in reality, unbelieving prayer for it dedicates itself to the will of the person doing the praying and not the will of God!

The Antidote also empowers us to understand more fully the truths that are contained in 1 John. When 1 John 1:9 is applied with the depth that is suggested through the use of The Antidote, the truths of 1 John suddenly come alive. Concepts within the epistle like experiencing Christian joy and fellowship (1 John 1), being able to keep the commands of God, having complete assurance that prayers will be answered all seem achievable (1 John 3–5). And perhaps one of the greatest benefits of 1 John can also be realized: experiencing complete assurance of salvation (1 John 5:10–13). In fact, The Antidote not only helps the Christian to understand 1 John. All of the writing of John and all of the writings of Scripture are also much more easily understood.

Chapter 18
R. B. and *The Antidote* (Revisited)

Remember the story of R. B. and Wildwood Church? What were the factors that positively affected Wildwood? What brought the church from a future that looked very grim to a future that looked very bright? The secret is in the application of The Antidote. Note how The Antidote changed the dynamics that were at work in the lives of the board members at Wildwood.

The board members of Wildwood heard the lectures which are contained in the chapters you have just read and they participated in small group sessions to explore how The Antidote might be applied to their lives. As the members of the board at Wildwood described how the forces of the abuse cycle had affected each one of them during the small group meetings, noticeable patterns became evident. Bryan, the son of R. B., described himself as a person who always found that he had to perform athletically. After all, his father had been one of the greatest athletes that had ever lived in the small town around Wildwood Church. And, his father was always very proud of Bryan's athletic endeavor. But, Bryan had failed, or so he felt. He had always dreamed of being an NBA star. But, he couldn't even get a basketball scholarship to a major university. He only received a partial scholarship from a small college. There was no possibility of becoming a part of the NBA. In fact, not even a try out was ever offered. He had felt that he was a failure. He then described himself as a person who could find importance in ministry. He had started a Bible study for young families. The church needed new, younger families. So, he felt this was a needed ministry. Few of these younger families, however, ever became a part of Wildwood Church. Why? The worship service of Wildwood was totally directed toward the needs of the old folks. So, Bryan's ministry importance was limited.

In addition, he had asked Pastor Harry if he could preach on several occasions. There was always an excuse given and no opportunity to preach was offered. When Bryan and the other members of the board attempted to make changes in the worship style, Pastor Harry had remained adamantly opposed to any changes, even changes that Bryan, his father R. B. and R. B.'s "crew" had suggested. The secret of Wildwood Church was becoming evident in the small group sessions. There was something of a war between Pastor Harry and R. B.'s "crew."

A life-long close friend of Bryan who was a member of the board also demonstrated a pattern that was evident when he described the effect of the abuse cycle in his own life. Bryan's friend, Joe, was also an athlete who found acceptance through high school athletics. He was on the same basketball team as Bryan. Joe had never dreamed of being an NBA star. He just wasn't that good a basketball player. But he had won notoriety for something quite interesting in basketball. He was the guard on the high school basketball team who was known for feeding the ball to Bryan. In fact, they were quite a duo: one making goals as the center of the team and the other feeding the ball to the center so that he could make the goals. He actually described the fulfillment he felt by making his friend, Bryan, the star of the team. He added that he also wanted to see Bryan successful in ministry. He also stated that he was resentful when Pastor Harry stood opposed to Bryan and the majority of the board members when they asked to change the style of the worship service.

R. B. also demonstrated a pattern. He described how his father had been an avid sports fan. He bought season tickets for the professional football team in his state and traveled to all of the games which were some distance away. He always took R. B. to the games. R. B. described these trips with sadness as he said these were the only times of closeness he ever had with his father. When he became a star athlete, his father was extremely proud of him. He never stopped bragging about R. B. to his friends and other members of the family. R. B. was delighted that his father was proud. But, R. B.'s glory days were eventually over. The opportunity to win his father's favor was lost when R. B. didn't make the Olympic wrestling team. R. B. added that he never felt closeness to his father after the failure to make the Olympics. R. B. said this with a deep expression of sadness.

The floodgate of tears began to open with Bryan. When Bryan was asked how he tried to win the favor of men, he described his ministry. And then, at the instigation of others in the group, he began to mention his athletic ability and his failure in athletics. Then, he recounted the favor he felt from his father during Little League as a child. He also related how much he wanted to win his father's love when he played basketball. Then, the tears came! For what might have been fifteen minutes, no one spoke. All that could be heard was the sobbing of Bryan. Why was Bryan sobbing? Because he regretted the waste of his life in trying to gain acceptance on the basis of athletics and ministry. He suddenly realized he was acceptable without having to be a star athlete or a great church leader. He was overwhelmed with gratitude toward Jesus. Jesus had given him complete acceptability. The relief he felt resulted in tears of regret and gratitude.

Then, Joe broke loose in tears. Bryan had explained his tears. Now, it was Joe's turn. Joe began to speak. He said he felt very bad for Bryan. He said that if he had only been able to help him with more assists in basketball, he might have been a candidate for the NBA. And then he realized, on his own without any prompting, that he had been trying to re-create the past by trying to help Bryan in ministry. He continued to weep, almost uncontrollably. It was very strange to see two adult men in tears. Why was Joe crying? He suddenly realized he was trying to gain acceptability by helping Bryan. He too was overwhelmed with gratitude toward Jesus. Jesus had given him acceptance whether he helped Bryan or didn't help Bryan. The two broke into an embrace. The atmosphere of the room was very somber.

But then it was R. B.'s turn. He started sobbing and sobbing and sobbing. Once again, after some time, he said that he had seen the connection between his own father and himself and how he had re-created the same pain in his own son's life. He also said that he now suddenly realized what he had also done to Joe. And so, the small group continued with three men sobbing. He added that he too was attempting to prove his value through his leadership position on the board. He was overwhelmed with regret because of what had happened in his own life and in the life of his son. And, he was overwhelmed with gratitude. Jesus gave him acceptance and this meant he could stop the frenzy of leadership attempts that were destroying his family and his church.

The other two men on the board were silenced by what they had seen. But everyone in the room realized what had caused the explosion at Church in the Wildwood. Slowly, each member of the board verbalized their understanding of what had happened. Multi-generational pain and a codependency between Bryan and Joe had ruled Wildwood. Each member of the board began to realize that The Antidote was the only way to heal themselves and the church that they loved. Each man began the process of confessing the individualized, secret ways he had been seeking the acceptance of men. In some cases, as in the case of R. B., public confession was appropriate. But no one had to push R. B. He confessed publicly during the next public Sunday morning worship. The effect was astounding. Wildwood Church was saved. As mentioned previously, members all over the church began to confess how they had been complicit in the problems of Wildwood. The healing of the Lord was on the way. James 5:16 was and is being fulfilled at Wildwood Church. "Therefore, confess your sins to one another, and pray for one another, so that you may be healed. The effective prayer of a righteous man can accomplish much."

It is important to note that a similar event took place among the five women that were part of my wife's small group at Wildwood Church. In fact, the leadership of the board and the wives of the board members provided leadership in seeing a healing that took place throughout the entire church. These are the same types of miracles we have regularly seen in both the US and Asia. This is the reason we are dedicated to teaching the principle of The Antidote. But there are many other, significant benefits of The Antidote. We will now turn our attention to what else is possible when The Antidote is applied to churches, mission groups, ministries of all kinds, and the lives of individual Christians.

At this time, the third small group session may begin. The goal of this session is to complete as much of exercise 2 as possible. Hopefully, question five of exercise 2 can be completed during this third session of the small groups.

Part 3
The Antidote: Recognizing and Correcting the System

"Moreover, they shall teach My people the difference between the holy and the profane, and cause them to discern between the unclean and the clean." Ezekiel 44:23

Chapter 19
Horror Story

The following story really happened. However, I have changed the circumstances and details in such a way so as to prevent the identification of the pastor, the church or the denomination that is involved. Any similarity with any series of events with which the reader is familiar is coincidental. Because I mention a denominational official in this story, it is necessary for me to share one fact about this story: This story did not occur in my own denomination. Sadly, I have seen stories similar to this one many times. This type of scenario is quite common, affecting many denominations and Christian organizations.

Several years ago, I had opportunity to meet Pastor Dan. He was introduced to me by Ted, a friend from a church I had previously served in an advisory capacity. Ted had recently joined Pastor Dan's church. Since I was in the process of raising support for the mission field, I asked Pastor Dan if he thought his church might be interested in supporting us. He presented the request to his mission board and his church. Valley Church became one of our supporting churches.

Over the next few years, I got to know Pastor Dan much better. We corresponded by email regularly between the US and Asia. After only a couple of years on the field, the emails from Pastor Dan revealed a problem at Valley Church. There were a group of individuals at the church, headed by one of the church's key leaders, who were regularly attacking Pastor Dan. Dan told me about the stinging criticisms that were spread in an attempt to undermine his ministry. Over the years, the problem worsened. Pastor Dan and I even had a couple of Skype calls between the continents. He really needed help, but I was too far away to do more than give some rather simple advice.

After these emails and Skype calls, I began suggesting to
Dan that he attempt to gain help from someone around his area,
particularly his denominational leadership. He contacted his local
denominational district superintendent. The superintendent, Greg,
dismissed his requests. Greg merely said that Dan was not handling
things properly and needed to "grow up" and stop "whining" about his
ministry problems. He also suggested that Dan needed counseling.
Greg met with Dan and the local antagonistic church leader and
openly supported the attacks on Dan. I then suggested Dan try to
find a Christian counselor. He tried in vain to find a good counselor.
He tried one counselor who gave little or no help as he absolutely
had no idea how to deal with the problems Dan was facing. Another
counselor was also little help. Neither of these counselors had ever
had any ministry other than counseling. They had no idea how to
help a pastor who was dealing with the types of problems Dan was
facing. One even expressed doubt in the veracity of Dan's account.
He couldn't believe a church would ever treat a pastor so badly. As
I listened to Dan's story, I realized he was becoming reactive. He
was seriously depressed and he potentially could explode in anger.
Fortunately, Dan never lost his temper, but I did suggest he find a
psychiatrist who could provide medical help. Dan, however, didn't
want to go to a psychiatrist. He felt that it would be an embarrassment
to admit to an unbelieving medical doctor how badly he was being
treated by those who claimed to be Christians. And so, Dan was
getting no help for the problems he was facing. I did my best to help
him, but distance prevented me from doing anything meaningful.
He needed someone who was physically with him to intervene in
some way. Dan's story is one of the reasons I decided to write my
first book on this subject and it is one of the reasons we decided to
broaden our ministry to reach into North America.

Finally, Dan's situation exploded. The antagonistic church leader
told the entire church that he had new and devastating charges to
make against Pastor Dan. The leader called an emergency business
meeting of the church. The district super joined the business meeting.
The leader told the congregation that he could not reveal the charges
in order to protect Dan from disgrace. Later, I learned from Ted that
the district super and the local church leader orchestrated the church

business meeting in such a way so as to prevent church members from identifying the true nature of the problem. Dan was fired! My friend also confirmed the stories which Dan told me. According to Ted, Dan was treated horribly by the church. Ted decided to leave Valley Church.

A few weeks after the firing, we were in the US. I called Dan. He told me the whole story about the charges against him. I knew that the charges were likely spurious as I had Dan's clear statement and the corroboration of Ted. And even if there was some truth regarding the charges against Dan, I knew something else. The way Greg and the local church leader were handling the situation did not, in any way, conform to Matthew 18:15–20 and 1 Timothy 5:19–21. It is my experience that when Scripture is violated, there is usually a reason. Often the open disregard of Scripture is not done to protect the victim; it is done to hide and protect the attacker. In other words, there was strong reason to question the behavior of the district super and the key leader of the church.

Then, Dan told me the detailed story, not only concerning the charges that produced his firing, but also how he had been treated by a group of leaders at Valley Church. He had been enduring unfair attacks for over twelve years. These attacks included constant criticism and false accusations which consisted of lies and half-truths. The biggest mistake Dan made was not leaving the church long before he was fired. This behavior demonstrated the possibility that Dan was a scripted victim who was enabling his antagonists by remaining in an untenable situation. However, in America, pastors can be controlled by the cultural value of what I call "Lone Ranger" mentality. All "Lone Ranger" pastors must find a way to become victorious over their circumstances no matter how hopeless they may seem. Consequently, many American pastors don't give up until it is too late.

Dan described how the situation worsened after his firing. He first tried to find employment in ministry somewhere new. But Greg and the local church leader impugned Dan's character whenever they had opportunity. The result was that Dan couldn't find work in any ministry of any kind. The only job he could find was working as a night stock clerk for a local grocery story. Dan's finances were in serious jeopardy. His wife and even his children took jobs to try to meet family needs. But something else was constantly plaguing Dan. He had been seeing a local doctor for back pain. Pain killers and therapy had been prescribed for several years. Finally, shortly after being fired, Dan could stand the pain no longer. He sought out a specialist who discovered that Dan had advanced kidney cancer. Dan endured surgery, chemo and radiation. Dan's children are among those whom I have described previously in *Toxic Church*. After seeing how their father and their entire family was treated by Valley Church, they now refuse to attend a local church (Luke 17:1–2).

Then, the story began to involve us in a surprising way. It was likely too late for us to do anything that might help both Dan and the church, but I decided to pray about any steps I might take. After prayer for some time, I decided to reach out to the church. After all, we were missionaries of the church and we specialized in dealing with conflicted situations in churches and mission teams. I called the church and asked to talk with anyone who might be leading the church at that time. I was shocked to discover that I was connected to the new pastor! After only a few months, the church had hired Dan's replacement. Normally, in this type of situation a church should have an intentional interim pastor who could help the church heal and correct any problems that remained. But this church, with the help of Greg, the district super, had hired a new pastor. How could Greg allow this to happen? Every rookie in ministry knows that you don't recommend a new pastor immediately after a church has fired a pastor! And I came to learn that the new pastor was a close friend of Greg! Of course, my mind began to consider several new reasons why Greg did not support Dan and why there was a new pastor so suddenly. But I knew I must reserve any judgment. So, I purposed to trust Greg and the new pastor.

When I first talked with the new pastor, Tom, I tried to get to know him. I learned that he was a young man who had served only one church, as a youth pastor for about seven years. He had no other ministry experience. As the conversation proceeded, I was surprised by what he told me. He constantly blamed Dan for every problem within the church. His criticism of Dan was endless. After listening to this man rail against Dan for about fifteen minutes, I finally was able to suggest something. I told him, "It is possible you are missing something. Would you get a copy of my book and read it? Could we talk after you have read the book?" The new pastor agreed and I told him I would call again in a month or so. It didn't take a month. He called me within about two weeks. The call was one-sided. He started railing against me! He told me how little I knew about ministry and how I didn't understand how evil a man Dan was. I said nothing in reply — absolutely nothing! He then changed the subject and spent at least another fifteen minutes telling me how gifted he was as a pastor. Basically, he bragged and bragged and bragged! He told me what a great preacher he was and what a gifted leader he was. He told me how he could make corrections in my book and how he could give me lessons on leadership and counseling churches. I couldn't believe what I was hearing. The frightening thing I noticed was that as he was describing his ministry at Valley Church in detail, I learned that he was making exactly the same mistakes which Dan had made — exactly the same mistakes! I said not one word as Tom went on and on and on. I finally had to cut him off. I said to him, "Tom, thank you for reading my book and for the time you have given to me." That was all I said, nothing more! Tom hung up the phone without saying another word. Two weeks later I received an unkind letter from Tom and the head of the mission committee. They had decided that the church would no longer support us!

Chapter 20
Step One: Removing the Log in Our Own Eyes

This "Horror Story" is a shocker. Unfortunately, stories like these are all too common. However, the question remains: How are stories like this one to be avoided? Necessary steps require recognizing and correcting the interplay of people that is at work in any troubled ministry. But, what are the steps that lead to a proper evaluation and correction of a system like that which existed at Valley Church? The following chapters contain an orderly progression of steps which can lead to a proper evaluation of any church, mission team or Christian ministry. Once an evaluation has been properly conducted, it is also possible to recommend steps that may correct the system and prevent future eruptions from occurring.

Without The Antidote, it is very difficult to evaluate conflict correctly in any church, ministry, or mission team. The reason: Without The Antidote, the possibility of being a people pleaser will dramatically skew any reasonable evaluation by an investigator concerning the cause of any relational problem. People pleasers, who by nature are seeking the acceptance of men, will invariably gravitate toward believing the story of those with the loudest and most numerous voices. Since the effect of the "identified patient" is often at work when conflict strikes an organization, there is likely a forceful group at work which offers acceptance to anyone who is examining a relational problem within any ministry. A group that is headed by an antagonist will invariably accuse the victim of causing the problem. And a person who has not applied The Antidote to his or her life will likely believe the account of those who offer the prize of human acceptance. It is so much easier to believe those in a church who offer acceptance to one who is examining a problem when the victim is likely no longer present or has been silenced into quiet acquiescence.

The result is predictable. The real problem is unnoticed. Those who caused the problem are left to run amok within the ministry. A repeat of the problem is likely. Anyone who will listen to the HP will hear the whole story with all the gory details about how evil the victim was and how the HP has saved the entire organization as a result of his or her heroic efforts to remove the problem through accusation and dismissal or forced resignation.

But something else happens when we apply The Antidote to our lives. Because we no longer need or seek the acceptance of men, we gain an ability to see men for what they are. We can see when someone is trying to control us by offering acceptance because we don't need the acceptance they offer. Simply put, we are then able to see how men attempt to manipulate and use us for their own gratification. We can also see when men do wrong. We are no longer tricked into accepting the account of an antagonist merely because he or she offers acceptance. Thus, we gain a perspective on the behavior of men which is no longer clouded by our own need to win the acceptance of others.

Also, remember that due to scripting, we tend to disregard our own dysfunctions. We tend to believe that our own behavior is the template or rule by which everyone else's behavior is to be judged. We see our own behavior as natural, normal and spiritual. Everything we do is viewed as right and proper human behavior. This means we are hopelessly predestined to ignore many of the flaws in others since their flaws are the same flaws that we ourselves possess. We are also hopelessly predestined to condemn others if they don't have the same flaws that we have. In addition, if I possess the script of hero-persecutor, I may see sins in others that do not exist. I do this because I have falsely believed that identifying the sins of others and punishing those sins brings value to myself. But, if I have confessed the attempt to gain the acceptance of men and learned to rely only on the acceptance of Jesus, I gain an ability no longer to attempt to identify sins in others in order to prove my own value. I also gain the ability no longer to identify sins in others which may not exist. And, I no longer need the acceptance of a hero-persecutor or the enablers of a hero-persecutor. Thus, I am better able to clearly identify the real wrong which men may be doing.

These truths require that we must first examine ourselves through the vehicle of The Antidote. The Antidote prevents us from making several errors in the evaluation of others. Only in first understanding our own dysfunctions are we then able to see the dysfunctions of others without the bias of our own personal script. Scripture puts it well:

> Or how can you say to your brother, Brother let me take out the speck that is in your eye, when you yourself do not see the log that is in your own eye? You hypocrite, first, take the log out of your own eye, and then you will see clearly to take the speck out of your brother's eye. Luke 6:42

The application of Luke 6:42 in our lives means that with complete and full examination of ourselves, an important benefit is derived. We gain an important balance as we can properly evaluate others without regard to whether or not they are able to give us human acceptance. This means we must escape the need to gain human acceptance. We must remove the log from our own eyes. And a principle way of doing this is by complete confession, included in the use of the principle of The Antidote.

Chapter 21
Step Two: Prayer

The Antidote is certainly a very important principle in learning how to evaluate a dysfunctional ministry system. But another equally important principle is prayer. It is important to remember that scripted behavior has power over each one of us throughout our lives. Even when we confess and forsake the default behavioral roles that we hope will win acceptance from men, those patterns of behavior are constantly at work within our lives. Our scripts constantly call us back to deviant behavior. Only with prayer is it possible not only to confess and end the tyranny of the script, but also to prevent it from suddenly appearing in our lives anew. So, if you are in a place where you need to evaluate the function or dysfunction of any church, mission organization or Christian ministry, the first step is the application of The Antidote. But the second step must include constant prayer that our scripts will not prevent us from making proper evaluation of any ministry. This need for prayer applies to a denominational leader, an intentional interim pastor, a pastor, an elder, or just a member of a church or ministry. The evaluation of a conflicted church or ministry must be empowered by persevering prayer.

Prayer should include many important requests including the need to avoid the temptation of accepting the labeling of the "identified patient." Any conflicted organization will constantly scapegoat others as the cause of the problem. Only with prayer is it possible to avoid listening to the multitude of voices who blame some other person or group of persons while finding themselves innocent. Pray that the truly guilty will betray themselves through telling statements that are often made in ignorance. It is also important to

123

pray that any steps the Lord may allow to correct the dysfunctional system will be filled with wisdom.

And one other factor must be considered if you are in a position in which you are asked to address a dysfunctional system and possibly correct it. Enlist the help of a prayer team that will assist you in the task of praying for your wisdom in the evaluation that you must make. The help of a group of prayer warriors has great power in enabling the work of correcting a dysfunctional system within any ministry. This should be viewed as a necessity.

Chapter 22
Step Three: Beware of Pilot Error

After reading the Horror Story, an obvious question must be asked. How could events like these take place? How could a pastor be blamed so repetitively without someone seeking to discover the entire truth of the matter? Who was wrong? Was it the pastor? Was it the leadership of the church? Was it both the pastor and the leadership of the church? Was it the denominational leader? Was the congregation responsible in some way? The membership of the church seemingly did nothing to discover the truth. The denominational leader certainly did little, if anything to help the church through the situation. And why was 1 Timothy 5:19–20 and Matthew 18:15–20 violated during the business meeting when Dan was fired?

There is a culprit at work. The culprit is something called "pilot error." A friend of mine, who is a retired United Airlines pilot, shared this story. He said that for several decades something occurred occasionally within the airline industry. Pilots would describe violent winds during takeoffs and landings that would suddenly put an airplane in great jeopardy. Over the years, dozens of airplane crashes were explained by surviving pilots as the result of these sudden, violent winds. Investigators dismissed the accounts of these surviving pilots. The verdict was usually the same: pilot error! These pilots were regularly fired as the result of these verdicts. Then, after a Delta flight suddenly took a nosedive during takeoff and crashed at DFW in the early 90s, investigators started paying closer attention to the data and eye witness accounts. They realized that there was a force, now labeled "wind shear," which can easily cause a plane to crash during violent thunder storms. Steps were taken to prevent future incidents by airline safety experts. Today, at all major airports around the world, there are wind shear indicators that warn pilots of dangerous winds during takeoff and landing. The result is that air safety has markedly improved and accounts of pilot error are now heard much less frequently. (I was personally appreciative of a pilot when I was on a flight in which the takeoff was aborted. The pilot announced that wind shear was at work. He told the passengers that he was going around to attempt takeoff a second time.)

But "pilot error" cries are still heard regularly within the ranks of Christian ministry. These cries cite the pastor, a key leader, or some other person or persons as the cause of the problem. The reason: the problem of the "identified patient." In the same way that Adam blamed Eve, making her the identified patient, we humans are totally willing to do the same thing. Many of us are willing to blame the innocent in order to transfer guilt from ourselves. And many others of us are willing to enable the antagonists of this world by allowing them to get away with it. It is so much easier to blame one person than it is to examine an entire group of individuals who may be involved. This is particularly true when everyone within the group is pointing at the victim as the cause of the problem. The result is that the innocent are often blamed when the problem is much bigger than that described by an antagonistic system.

How is the problem of pilot error corrected? When "identified patient" mentality is at work, there is a likelihood that the problem is much deeper than blaming one person or a group of people. Every ministry team, mission group or church must be examined in light of the possibility that the "dance," which was described earlier, is at work. If there is a "dance" pattern at work within a group, those who have the same dance will be automatically accepted while those who do not have the same dance will be rejected. In other words, a person can be victimized for reasons that have nothing to do with the truth. And others can believe the attackers for the same reason.

Be aware of other factors that can affect one who is investigating the causes of conflict. Could long term relationships between antagonists and investigators cloud the judgment of an investigator? Could an absence of personal experience on the part of an investigator be a problem? Never forget: Pastor Tom really had very limited experience. And, he undoubtedly had little or no experience with being attacked (although that will likely change as his church is still very troubled and he was and is too naïve to realize the danger that he faces).

Another difficulty in eliminating the problem of pilot error is understanding the behavior of the victim. Anyone who is victimized repetitively, no matter how strong, will eventually become reactive. A reactive person will become depressed and possibly demonstrate anger in statements or demeanor. When this occurs, the investigator must be smart enough to ask a simple question: Is the behavior of the victim the cause of the problem or the result of the problem?

It is also important to consider the behavior of the leadership of any church or ministry team. Certain questions need to be asked. Why did the team call the pastor or leader who was attacked? Is it possible that there was a script at work in which certain leaders were looking for viable victims? (Recall, Pastor Tom's mistakes were the same as Pastor Dan's. Why was Tom called? Is it possible that scripts were at work in which Tom was called because he looked like the next viable victim?)

And when victims make mistakes, and all of us make mistakes, were these mistakes corrected Biblically by those in leadership? Failure to confront Biblically is actually an enabling function for it allows a victim to behave in such a manner that problems grow. Then, attacks may occur when confrontation could have prevented the problem. There is a difference between an attack and a confrontation. Attacks are confrontations that don't follow Biblical rules for correcting a person in error. Biblical confrontation corrects when sin issues are present and Biblical rules for confrontation are followed. Biblical confrontation may prevent attacks because one of the sources of the attack has been corrected.

In addition, did the leadership of the church or ministry fail to protect the victim when being attacked? When someone is not protected during an attack, the likelihood is that the leaders were behaving according to an enabling script, allowing the attack to continue when it should have been stopped.

In the same way that the leadership of a ministry team or church must be examined, so must every member of a conflicted church or ministry. When members of a local church do not step in and insist that Scriptural steps are enforced when someone is accused, the members have also made themselves enablers. Don't forget: The members of Valley Church let the leadership of the church get away with failing to identify the sins of Pastor Dan and they failed to insist that Matthew 18:15–20 and 1 Timothy 5:19–21 be enforced. This means that not only were the leaders of Valley Church at fault; the members were also. And, though we don't have complete information, Pastor Dan was also at fault in at least one way: He didn't leave the church when he should have left!

These factors lead to one simple truth: Conflict is never a one-person problem! It isn't even a leadership problem! It is a problem of the entire organization, church, or ministry. It is a system wide problem. Whenever someone is blamed while others are exonerated, there is a certainty: The entire system is flawed in some way. Remember, everyone at Valley Church was willing to escape culpability by blaming Pastor Dan. Denominational leader Greg was willing to sacrifice Pastor Dan. The church leaders were certainly willing to sacrifice Pastor Dan. And the members of Valley Church were certainly willing to allow Pastor Dan to be sacrificed. Questions need to be asked about a church that has experienced conflict. Why did Valley call Dan as their pastor? Is it possible that he was chosen because an antagonist needed someone to victimize and Dan appeared vulnerable? Did the members of the church fail to correct or protect Dan when the problems first became evident? Were there conflicts within the church before Dan arrived? Did the church membership and leadership fail to follow Dan's leadership?

Pastor Dan was also guilty in some ways which may not be identified. He stayed for twelve years in a church that was attacking him. He either didn't properly confront his attackers or he didn't leave when Biblical confrontation did not eliminate the problem. In addition, Dan did not properly disciple new leaders. He didn't slowly change the leadership into a body of more Godly leaders through proper discipleship. And most important: Dan didn't keep looking for help from others in ministry when Greg failed to help him. He failed to continue to seek a Christian counselor who could help him. (A good counselor could have determined if Dan was a scripted victim who was allowing the attacks upon himself because of bizarre scripting needs). He failed to get the help of a psychiatrist. And, he failed to leave despite all the signs that he was serving a toxic church. These factors all indicate that Dan was probably a true enabler of the attacks that were made against him.

These factors lead to a simple and very important conclusion: Never accept an evaluation of a conflicted church or ministry which exonerates some while blaming others. Never, never, never make this mistake. The problem is always, always, always a system wide problem. Even those who are seemingly completely innocent have in some way enabled the problem by allowing it to continue. When antagonists are allowed to attack, they are not the only ones who are at fault. Each person who did not act to prevent the attack was in some way a part of the problem. By failing to act in the face of conflict, enablers are just as responsible as the individuals who actually create the problem. And even victims bear responsibility when they don't Biblically confront or leave when they are being attacked. A good investigator will take all of these factors into account.

Chapter 23
Step Four: Recognize the Decision that Has to be Made

Decisions have to be made as the result of any investigation of a conflicted church or ministry. Primarily one of three decisions must be made by any professional who is investigating a troubled ministry. The first is the least confrontational approach. This approach is one in which an intentional interim pastor, a pastor or ministry leader determines to disciple the current leadership of the church or ministry. The goal is to slowly correct any problem scripts that may be creating conflict within the ministry. Along with this method, the church or organization constitution may be changed in such a way that power is given to those who might prevent future problems. The strength of this approach is that it creates little rancor among the members and leaders of a troubled church or Christian organization. The weakness is that it may fail to correct the dysfunction that troubles the church or ministry due to the fact that the scripting of the ministry leaders is so strong that discipleship may fail to bring about timely resolution of the problem. This approach is generally not advisable unless the conflict appears to be rather minimal and current leaders demonstrate considerable teachability.

The second approach is one in which an intentional interim pastor, pastor or leader asks for a suspension of the current leadership of the church or ministry until such a time as an evaluation of what occurred can be completed. The suspension is usually temporary with a time limit. The strength of this method is that it also creates a lower level of rancor among church or ministry leaders. However, the weakness is that it may only postpone the inevitable decision that changes in leadership are necessary. If leaders are not restored in a timely manner, considerable difficulty is possible. In addition, it is hard to ask leaders to step aside until the process of discipleship produces benefit. Discipleship takes time. If the intent is to make current leaders less dysfunctional, the impatience of the ministry or church membership may prevent the completion of the task to make leaders more functional. This approach should only be used if an investigator believes the problem can be corrected with the current leadership of the ministry and in a relatively short period of time.

The third approach is the most difficult one to impose. This approach asks the congregation or ministry to dismiss current leaders (Matthew 7:20–23). The ministry or church membership is also asked to allow for considerable time in which either new leaders are found and trained or current leaders are retrained. In the meantime, an alternative method of governance can be implemented such as congregational rule or rule by several committees. The weakness of this approach is that it will produce the greatest amount of rancor. The strength is that this approach provides the greatest opportunity for functional leaders to be placed into the church or ministry.

Whichever approach is taken, it is important for any professional to understand there is a potential for war when attempting to correct a dysfunctional local church or ministry. Don't forget what my friend, who is a retired denominational official, told me, "The key ingredient for anyone in ministry (including an intentional interim) is that he doesn't care." In other words, the intentional interim or conflict resolution team must not be afraid of conflict or the lack of acceptance from the members and leaders of a troubled organization or church. This is a quality which the investigators of conflict can receive through the application of The Antidote in their own lives. So, those who would address conflicted churches or ministries must be prepared to make decisions, even the possibly unpopular ones.

It is also important for any professional to take similar steps when entering into the ministry of any local church or Christian ministry, whether conflicted or not. Discipleship of leaders is always an imperative. When leaders are properly nurtured, destructive scripts and roles are controlled within the leader or potential leader's life. In this case, the problem of conflict is dramatically reduced. This is one of the reasons Jesus told us to "Go and make disciples" (Matthew 28:19–20).

And even those who are not involved in the leadership of a local church or ministry have decisions to make. They too must evaluate where culpability of a conflicted church or ministry exists. If a member of a conflicted church does not Biblically confront those who are the primary cause of problems, that member has become an enabler of the problem. And if there is no opportunity to confront Biblically, and the person determines to stay in the conflicted church or ministry, the net effect is that the person still is an enabler of the dysfunction. In other words, the layman or non-leader of any local church or Christian organization must determine if he or she has the power to confront those who are the proponents of conflict and whether they will remain in a conflicted organization should confrontation fail and dysfunction continue.

Chapter 24
Step Five: Learn How to Identify an Antogonist

Antagonists are not hard to identify. There are keys which help to identify antagonistic and enabling personalities. No one of these keys can be used to identify with certainty those who will cause or enable conflict within a church or Christian ministry. However, when several of these keys are apparent in a person's life, the likelihood that this person is either a hero persecutor or an enabler of a hero persecutor is quite high.

The first of these keys is the identification of dysfunction within the family or ministry of the person who may be the primary cause of conflict. First Timothy 3:4–5 indicates that the household of a potential elder must be examined carefully for dysfunction. There is a reason: Where there is dysfunction, the abuse cycle is also at work. And when the abuse cycle is at work, the addictive forces which may also produce a scripted hero-persecutor and enablers of hero persecutors are also at work. It is also important to define the word "household" within 1 Timothy. A household included not only immediate family members, but also grandchildren and great grandchildren along with their family members. A household also included servants, their immediate family members, and once again, their extended family members. Servants within a household are akin to workmates in today's society. As an example of the possible size of a household, Genesis 14:14 gives an indication of the size of Abraham's household. In this text, we are told that Abraham's household included 318 fighting men. And this number reflects the number of men after Abraham's household had been divided first in Haran between Abraham and his brother and then in Canaan between Abraham and Lot. These 318 did not include men too old or too young to fight and no women were included. So, Abraham's original household may have included several thousand. Though Paul wrote 1 Timothy in Roman times, the Roman *pater familia* could also include hundreds and possibly thousands of individuals. This means that the concept of the household includes not only immediate and extended family members, but it also includes those under the charge of a person in the workplace and wherever a person may congregate with others. When dysfunctional behavior is found within a person's household, it does not guarantee that dysfunctional scripts are also evident within that person's life. After all, what person does not have some dysfunctional member within his family or within his charge in the workplace? But, it does indicate that greater examination of a person with dysfunctional household members is warranted.

A second simple key is to examine who the "identified patient" may be. Recall that the identified patient is likely not the real patient. So, if a person is known to identify others as a problem, the likelihood is that the person doing the identifying is the real problem.

A third key, similar to the second, is understanding the necessity of confession. Hero-persecutors don't confess; they indicate others should confess. Their means of proving their own value is to identify and correct others. For this reason, they seldom are willing to confess. And when they do confess, it is likely only a ploy to maintain their position of being hero or leader of an organization. So, if confession is warranted in any particular situation and a person steadfastly refuses to confess, that person is likely the dysfunctional person who needs to be corrected.

A fourth key is identifying anyone who has told a lie, even a little "white" lie. Lies are often told to convince others that the person who is lying is not culpable in any way for a problem that may have surfaced. Therefore, when a person is caught in a lie, that person must be examined very carefully as the probable cause of any conflict (see John 8:44).

A fifth key is noticing the person who wants to be known as the "hero." As all seasoned pastors know, it is important to recognize that the person who says, "Pastor, I will always be on your side," is also the person who is most likely to betray the pastor given the right opportunity. Another old proverb, shared among pastors, is, "Watch out for the one who meets you at the train." Today, the proverb might read, "Watch out for the one who meets you at the plane." But, why is it wise for a new pastor to watch out for the one who first greets the pastor and offers support? Because that person is also the one who may want to be known as the hero of the church; the one who wants to say to the pastor that he is the one who can be depended upon if some difficulty arises. Heroes like to be known for their ability to be a hero. So, they tend to find ways to posture themselves as heroes to the right person at the right time. And, heroes love to use the word "I" when they declare themselves as the hero. As an example, in Isaiah 14:13–14, Satan said the word "I" five times in an attempt to prove his importance. Hero-persecutors do the same thing. They love to use the word "I." So, listen carefully for the use of this word. It will betray a hero-persecutor very quickly.

A sixth key is the identification of a person who wants to avoid any type of intervention or examination of a conflicted church or ministry. Statements like this are frequently heard: We don't need the help of so and so as we are not troubled. Or, the person may say: We don't need the help of so and so because we all know who the cause of the problem is and we have dealt with the problem. And if a person feigns support for an investigation and then fails to follow through or undermines the investigation in some way, that person is most likely an antagonist. The reason is simple: A hero-persecutor fears that any serious investigation may identify themselves as the real source of the problem. When this happens, the hero-persecutor will likely be demoted in some way and the means of winning the favor of men has been lost. So, a hero-persecutor will use any clever means necessary to undermine a serious investigation.

A seventh key is the identification of a person who wants to be the leader. They are the people who always stand in the corner with their hands raised, saying "Pick me; pick me!" They will always enlist the help of others in winning any key leadership position. They may also be those dedicated to learning leadership principles. There is nothing wrong with understanding leadership, but what if the reason for learning leadership principles is so the acceptance of men can be won? If so, this is a person who is also likely the possible cause of a problem within a church or organization. Though understanding leadership principles does not necessarily mean a person is an antagonist, seldom are antagonists unwilling to study these principles. The reason: If they can get others to do what they want through the use of leadership principles, they will also win more acceptance through a greater following.

An eighth key is recognizing when someone fails in an ability to follow others. Followers give leaders the ability to lead as is demonstrated in Joshua 1 (further examination of this chapter will be conducted in a later chapter). In God's economy leaders don't get to rule others (Luke 22:24–26). The only way they can lead is if the followers choose to follow the leader. So, if an individual cannot follow in the simplest tasks, the question must be asked as to why. Is it possible that the person is jealous of those who lead? Is it possible that the person wants to assert themselves and thus win the acceptance of others? Jesus stated that one of the required qualities of a disciple was: "Follow Me" (Matthew 4:19 & John 21:19). A person who cannot follow in the simplest tasks may be demonstrating an inability to share the spotlight with others. For this reason, those who seem unable to follow others may possess dysfunctional scripts.

The ninth key to recognizing an antagonist is to note when someone is unwilling to obey 1 Timothy 5:19–20 or Matthew 18:15–20. The reason these Biblical injunctions are often ignored is that the antagonist wants the freedom to attack the victim without having to obey the controls which are contained in these passages.

Finally, the tenth key to recognizing an antagonist is vengeful behavior. This is behavior which seeks to destroy others. It is not just anger. Anger is the normal reaction to injustice. Victimized individuals can be very angry when attacked. Vengeful behavior is not demonstrated only by anger; it is demonstrated by a determination to get revenge, to hurt a person in some vindictive manner. After all, the antagonist says to himself, this person has destroyed my ability to gain acceptance. They say to themselves that this person must be repaid for the evil they have done. And so, vengeful acts follow. This was exactly the same behavior that Cain showed toward his brother, Abel. For this reason, it is one of the most important keys to identifying an antagonist.

Chapter 25
Step Six: The Simple Trick of Listening

Listening to what people say within a conflicted or potentially conflicted church or ministry is the simplest way to identify the hero persecutors and the enablers of hero persecutors within that organization. There is a simple reason: Antagonists and their cohorts are trying to win a following. To do this, they love to brag! So, a simple technique is to ask questions of the leaders and other members of a particular church or ministry. If an investigator has an identified position within a church or ministry, such as pastor or interim pastor, interviews with key individuals can be easily arranged. But even if a person is just a member of the church or ministry, questions can be asked in an informal manner. When enough individuals are interviewed, a clear picture of the hero persecutors and their enablers can be recognized. Whole dysfunctional systems within a church or ministry can be identified in this way. If possible, it is wise to write down the answers to questions that are asked during the interview. If this is not practical, recording the answers immediately after an interview is very important in order to help recognize the members of a system that have been revealed through the discussion. Prayer before each interview is critical. Pray that clues will be revealed regarding who the members of a dysfunctional system may be.

Several ministry organizations recommend interviewing members of churches and Christian ministries in order to analyze those ministries, particularly organizations that attempt to assess local churches or ministries. There are several key questions that help identify the strengths and weaknesses of any church or Christian ministry. These questions can also be used to help the personal growth of individuals within a particular organization. Here is a list of potential questions that can be asked of various members of a church or ministry. These questions are not exhaustive. Other questions can also be asked. But these questions can provide a start in learning about the strengths and weaknesses of any organization.

1. Share briefly your faith story. How did you come to know the Lord?
2. When did you begin attending XYZ church? When did you become a part of XYZ ministry?
3. What attracted you to XYZ?
4. What is your involvement at XYZ?

When a local church or Christian ministry has demonstrated conflict, the questions that can be asked provide significant insight into the workings of the system within that particular church or organization. Here is a list of potential questions that can be asked of leaders and members of a conflicted church or ministry. Once again, this list is not exhaustive. Other questions can be added. But the answers to these questions begin the process of identifying those who are part of a dysfunctional system within an organization. And once again, the answers to these questions need to be recorded in writing either during the interview or as soon after the interview as possible.

1. Who do you see as the person or persons who caused the problem?
2. Who do you see as the person or persons who demonstrated skill in solving the problem?
3. Who was a key leader in addressing the problem?
4. Who assisted the key leader in addressing the problem?
5. Do you think the problem was handled properly?
6. What did you do to help?
7. Did you, in any way, contribute to the problem?

A third set of questions can help when a local church or ministry has demonstrated little or no conflict. The answers to these questions can identify potential dysfunctional systems within the organization. Once again, answers to these questions are not exhaustive. Other questions can be asked. And once again, the answer to these questions should be recorded in writing either during or immediately following the interview.

1. What do you see as a potential problem within this organization?
2. Who do you see as the person/persons who might cause a problem within this ministry?
3. Who do you see as the person/persons who might be able to correct this potential problem?
4. Is there one particular leader whom you see as critical in addressing this potential problem?
5. What could you do to help should this problem arise?
6. Have you done anything that might contribute to this potential problem?

After conducting these interviews with a significant number of leaders and members of a local church or Christian ministry, analyzing the answers becomes very important. The interviewer must ask himself or herself these questions:

1. Did anyone introduce himself or herself to you as a person you could always trust? (Remember: Scripted heroes often try to win acceptance this way)
2. Was anyone opposed to your investigation? Did anyone demonstrate opposition to your findings once they became evident?
3. Who was willing to point the finger at others, but never take any responsibility for a potential or actual problem?
4. Did you uncover the evidence of lies that were told through conflicting answers? (Remember: Lies are often told to deflect culpability and blame others).
5. How did individuals identify groups as you asked who might be a help or a hindrance in addressing a particular problem? (This is a clear indication of the members of a functional or not so functional system).
6. Though difficult to ask questions about family relationships, are you personally aware of any dysfunctional family relationships within the leadership of a local church or ministry? (These

are the signs of the presence of the abuse cycle and possible dysfunctional roles).

After analyzing the answers to the questions that were gained during the interview process, it is necessary to attempt to identify the healthy and not so healthy members of the local church or ministry. The question of whether there is a dysfunctional system within the church or ministry must be considered. And if there may be a dysfunctional system within the ministry, who are the likely HPs and enablers of HPs? This will require a great deal of prayer, asking for the help of Lord in understanding how the system within the organization functions. Decisions that are made by faith will become necessary. Without the determination to decide by faith how the members of a potentially destructive system operate, it will become impossible to address potential or actual problems within any church, mission or ministry organization. However, once these decisions have been made, the process of developing a strategy to address conflict or potential conflict within the church or organization is possible.

Chapter 26
Step Seven: Dealing with a Dysfunctional Ministry: Lead!

Joshua 1 contains one of the most important of all the leadership principles within Scripture. In this chapter, a miracle is described. God instructed Joshua to be strong and courageous. Joshua obeyed. He challenged the people to cross the Jordan and begin the conquest of Canaan. The people of Israel followed Joshua. The succeeding miracles resulted in the birth of the nation of Israel. However, Joshua would never have known if the people would have followed if he had not determined to lead. This points out something very important to all of God's leaders. If a leader doesn't lead, the leader doesn't learn if the people will follow. And if a leader doesn't lead, the miracle which God offers may not be realized. When applying this simple principle within a conflicted local church, mission group, or ministry, the application is simple: Lead! Without leading the people, a leader never learns if the people will follow. And the leader may never see correction and healing within a conflicted local church or ministry. Conflicted organizations need leaders who develop strategies to correct the problems that are evident. Without leadership, nothing happens. Conflict only repeats itself due to the addictive forces that cause scripts to reappear with greater intensity and frequency. Leaders develop strategies to address conflict and the scripts which cause conflict. Though a leader can't force people to follow, a leader will never know if the people will follow if leadership is not exerted. And if the people follow, the potential for correcting conflicted organizations is real. God may bless and heal a conflicted organization, allowing it to return to the purpose for which it is called.

In chapter 23 of this study on recognizing and correcting a dysfunctional church or ministry, various possible solutions were considered. After taking the steps cited in the previous chapters of this book, a leader must then determine to lead by following one of the steps listed in chapter 23. To refuse to take decisive action when addressing a conflicted system within a Christian ministry guarantees that it will continue to behave in dysfunction, causing future conflicts and problems of every sort. There were three possible solutions that were suggested in Chapter 23. One was to disciple the current leadership of a conflicted ministry, hoping to affect significant change. A second was to ask that current leadership is suspended until an analysis of a problem is conducted. This second step involves instituting temporary methods of governance until leaders are properly mentored and trained. A third was to dismiss current leadership. This step also involves developing new methods of governance until new leaders are properly trained. The decision as to which of these suggestions is applied must be based on the severity of the problem. Scripted behavior changes very slowly and often only when properly confronted. If the evidence of serious scripts within the leadership of an organization is present, it is best to find and train new leaders. If the scripting of current leadership is not intense, a temporary suspension is possible. If the scripting of current leadership appears relatively mild, it is possible to train current leaders to function more properly. After determining how intense the scripting of a ministry's leadership is, a leader must then take corrective steps.

It is also then necessary to determine what individuals within a ministry are functioning properly or not so properly. Some individuals may need to be removed from leadership, but it is not always necessary to change the entire leadership of a conflicted ministry. But how is it determined if an organization has reached the point that the entire leadership needs to be removed? One of the ways to do this is by first examining the ways to identify the existence of a hero persecutor as suggested in chapter 24. Another way is to use the listening methods suggested in chapter 25 to identify the highly dysfunctional members of a leadership team. Once these individuals have been identified, a simple test can be conducted. First, the dysfunctional leader or leaders must be asked to remove themselves based upon problems that have been noted. If the highly dysfunctional leaders refuse to remove themselves, the next step is to suggest to the entire leadership of the organization that this person or persons should be removed either temporarily or permanently. A highly scripted hero persecutor may not yet have been able to create a fully dysfunctional system, complete with enablers of every sort. If the entire leadership is willing to heed this advice to remove a particular leader, the hero persecutor and other dysfunctional leaders have not yet been able to develop a fully dysfunctional system within the leadership of the church or ministry. But if the entire leadership is unwilling to allow this step, the hero persecutor has been successful in creating an enabling system within the leadership of the organization. The entire leadership team must be considered as dysfunctional at that point. Homeostasis has likely set in. Even if a hero persecutor is removed, the remaining members of the team will only recruit a new hero persecutor causing the leadership to promote continued conflict. So, recommending the removal of a hero persecutor has the potential of revealing how developed a dysfunctional system may be within a church or ministry.

The task of requalifying leaders or training new leaders is always necessary when conflict occurs within a local church or ministry. Certain Biblical requirements must be enforced when training or requalifying leaders. First Timothy 3 clearly indicates church leaders must have functional families. If a leader's household shows signs of dysfunction, that leader should be asked to resign until such time as the household issue is addressed. First Timothy 3 and Titus 1 also require that leaders must be involved in the ministry of the Word. Those who refuse to be involved in actual ministry, should be asked to resign. Those who are willing should be taught through a good discipleship program to be faithful witnesses, counselors, teachers and preachers. Then, leaders should be expected to take positions in which the function of the ministry of the Word is insured during their time as part of a leadership team.

Those who have been removed from leadership must be given help, particularly those who were dismissed as a result of the dysfunction within the church or organization. If a pastor or leader has been forced from the ministry, professional Christian counseling must be provided for that person. Reconciliation meetings can be conducted, but only if those who attend are all willing to confess how they contributed to the problem. Without the willingness to confess on the part of all who attend reconciliation meetings, the meeting will become nothing more than finger pointing sessions in which those who have been victimized will only be victimized again.

Those who remain in the leadership of a conflicted church or ministry must also receive proper care. Those with marginally troubled families, should be offered Christian counseling. Discipleship programs which include learning how to be ministers of the Word must also be offered. If evidence of problems surface in which the Biblical qualifications of 1 Timothy 3 and Titus 1 are not being obeyed, that person should be asked to resign from leadership until these issues are completely addressed.

These steps require leadership on the part of those who intervene in conflicted ministries. If a leader with an opportunity to intervene fails to do so, that person has become an enabler of the problem. As has been noted, it is sometimes necessary to take dramatic steps to correct a conflicted ministry. A leader who has the opportunity to intervene in a conflicted church or ministry may be forced to refuse to help a ministry that will not accept his suggestions which will correct the problem. As an example, a denominational leader may have to refuse to help a local church that has dismissed its pastor in the task of finding a new pastor. The same denominational leader may be threatened by those within the conflicted local church. In fact, it is even possible that a denominational leader who refuses to enable a dysfunctional local church or ministry may be personally attacked. If the leader is paid in some way by the conflicted church or ministry, the leader may be forced to resign. The leader may even be fired. However, to fail to correct the dysfunctional behavior of the leadership of a particular church or ministry only insures a continuation of the problem. Due to the forces of addiction, future eruptions with more intensity and with more frequency are certain. In addition, even if a denominational leader resigns, the problem may be passed to his successor. (In fact, leaders often inherit problems from predecessors who failed to address a problem.)

And there is the potential that the problem will infect other ministries within an organization. A troubled church within a denomination may cause the types of problems which are evident within that particular church to be tolerated in other churches. Thus, the conflicted local church or ministry can cause the problem not only to become a homeostatic one in which problems continue within that particular church or ministry; it can also cause the problem to actually metastasize, causing other organizations or churches within the denomination or organization to become dysfunctional as well. This all means one thing: Leaders must lead! Without the willingness to deal with the problems of conflicted local churches and ministries, problems will continue and grow. This last step is not an easy one. But there is no easy answer. The challenge can only be presented. A question remains: Will those who read these words be willing to confront conflicted local churches, mission organizations, and other Christian ministries?

But . . . therein lies the value of The Antidote. If a leader is defined by the love of Jesus and not by the need to find acceptance from men, that leader will not be tyrannized by those who threaten. In fact, dysfunctional individuals lose all power over the leader. An often-recognized definition of a leader is "a self-defined person with a non-anxious presence." Perhaps, this definition can be changed slightly. A leader is "a Jesus defined person with a non-anxious presence." This is achievable for those who take the time to analyze themselves and apply the principle of The Antidote to their own lives. And when this happens, the somewhat frightening steps that have been suggested in this chapter become doable. Troubled local churches, mission organizations, and Christian ministries of all kinds can then be delivered from the destructive forces of conflict!

Small group sessions should be ongoing at this point. Exercise 2 should be completed at this time and exercise 3 should be almost completed.

Part 4
The Antidote and Biblical Confrontation

"And if your brother sins, go and reprove him in private…"
Matthew 18:15–20

Chapter 27
The Controntation Conunbrum

Confrontation is often the only answer for the problem of stopping those who cause conflict. Conflict resolution techniques are often very valuable. However, when individuals are addicted to destructive scripts, the benefit of conflict resolution is often quite limited. Addicted individuals will often resist changes in behavior which will eliminate problems of conflict. The addict may even resent those who ask him or her to change. Those who persecute others or allow the persecution of others often see their dysfunctional behavior as natural, normal and spiritual. The addict may emphasize those Scripture verses which seem to confirm dysfunction while ignoring or giving little attention to Scripture verses which correct dysfunction. Thus, the dysfunctional addict often becomes unteachable regarding failed behavioral patterns. When forced, the addicted individual may feign change for a time, but when the opportunity arises, a return to addicted patterns of behavior will occur. In this case, the only real solution is to apply ways to circumvent the problems which are presented by the addicted individual. The answer is strong, Biblical confrontation.

There are several excuses as to why we don't confront. Culture is often used as an excuse for failing to confront. As an example, those in the West have individualistic cultures. Westerners give each individual the right to make the major decisions of life. As I describe American values to Asians, I frequently describe America this way: "America is the land of the free, the home of the brave, the rugged individualist, one man, one vote. We shoot the Indian. We conquer the West. I am the Lone Ranger." As a result of these values, individuals are largely unaccountable to others regarding the way they live their lives. We Americans say, "Do your own thing," and "Who am I to say what is right or wrong in another person's life?" We Americans also fear retribution from those who might be confronted. After all, since each person has the right to make his own decisions, any person whom we confront has the right to be angry with us for confronting them. So, Westerners and particularly Americans don't confront.

In the East, cultural excuses for failing to confront evil are also made. Many parts of Asia are controlled by Confucian values. These values include a necessity for unity, order, harmony, and respect for others, particularly for those who are older or more learned. A culture influenced by Confucian values is a collectivistic culture. Individual decisions are always made with a view to how the entire family or society may be affected. Confrontation is always very risky for it endangers the unity and harmony of those within the people group of the confronter. So, it is often avoided, particularly when directed at those who are older. Recently, in Thailand, I asked an Asian teaching assistant if he could ever confront me. This man is about thirty years younger than I am. He replied that he could never confront me! Closely akin to those with a Confucian worldview are those from tribal cultures. The tribal elder controls every aspect of tribal culture. If you are not the tribal elder, confronting another within the tribe is tantamount to usurping the position of the tribal elder. In addition, every decision is made with a view to how it will be accepted by the tribal elder and by the members of the tribe. So, confrontation is seldom done in tribal or Confucian cultures.

However, the real impediment to applying Biblical confrontation is quite simple: No matter what our cultural context, all humans fear losing the approval and acceptance of others due to the forces of the Fall. Our culture develops around this fear. The result is that Biblical confrontation is either ignored or poorly applied in every culture. Because of this controlling reason that confrontation is avoided, the application of The Antidote is necessary. When the application of The Antidote is completed in a person's life, the fear of losing acceptance no longer tyrannizes. A person can then apply Biblical confrontation and prevent many problems of dysfunction from causing conflict with a ministry or local church.

Confrontation should not be controlled by Western or Eastern culture. It should be controlled by Bible culture! The real problem is that confrontation, when it is attempted or tried, is often done incorrectly. It is done through the filter of Western or Eastern or Tribal culture. The result is predictable: Confrontation fails. When we understand how Scripture teaches us to confront, a new perspective is gained—a God perspective which demonstrates how confrontation is done in such a manner that it avoids many of the pitfalls that exist in various cultural contexts. Bible confrontation is loving confrontation. A good Biblical confronter can confront in such a way that the person being confronted doesn't even know he is being confronted. Recently, I was teaching a class on confrontation is Asia. Every student gave reasons why confrontation was difficult. The excuses were related to tribal cultural norms and Confucian worldview. I asked the students if they thought the president of the seminary where I was teaching had the ability to confront. Without exception, each student stated that they knew this Asian seminary president could confront. Later, during a class break, I had opportunity to talk to this Asian president in the presence of many of the students from the class. I asked him if he had difficulty confronting others. He stated in a very typical low key, low volume, loving Biblical manner: Never! He went on to say that confrontation is easy if it is done the Bible way!

Scripture clearly teaches the principle of the confrontation of evil. The evidence is clear in passages like Proverbs 9:7–9; Matthew 18:15–20; Luke 17:1–4; 1 Timothy 5:1–2, and numerous and uncountable passages elsewhere in Scripture. The reason Scripture commands us to confront evil is due to the nature of evil and the nature of the devil who promotes evil. The Greek word for the devil is *diabolos*. This word comes from two Greek words: *dia* and *bolos*. *Dia* means "through" in English. *Bolos* means "to throw" in English. Thus, the Devil is the one who "throws through." He attacks; he accuses; he slanders; he persecutes and he eliminates his foes by clever tactics. Through the forces of the Fall of Man, he is able to use any one of us in the task of harming others. He accomplishes this through destructive, addictive scripts which we use in an attempt to validate ourselves and gain the acceptance of others. Simply put:

Satan won't stop unless we take Scriptural steps to stop him! And the primary means of correcting those who are being used by Satan to harm others is Biblical confrontation!

In fact, the greatest way to love a scripted, dysfunctional person is with confrontation. When an alcoholic is unwilling to admit his or her problem, those who are around the alcoholic must confront him or her. It is an act of love. Al Anon and other organizations have learned that it is also necessary to confront not only the alcoholic, but also those who enable the alcoholic. In exactly the same manner, not only must hero persecutors be confronted, but also those who enable the hero persecutor. Biblical confrontation methods must be implemented if the problem of evil within any local church or Christian ministry is to be prevented. So, we now turn our attention to understanding principles of Biblical confrontation.

Chapter 28
The Methodology of an Attack

One of the keys to understanding Biblical confrontation is recognizing when and how it should be applied. There are various phases of an accusation or an attack and each phase must be handled differently. Before suggesting a step by step Biblical procedure, it is important to recognize the way these accusations and attacks take place. Though the progression of an attack can happens at different paces and with some slight variations, generally there are four phases in an attack. I call these four phases the secret phase, the public phase, the serious phase and the reactive phase.

The secret phase is exactly what it suggests. No one, sometimes not even the primary antagonist, knows that an attack is brewing. It usually begins with the antagonist/HP noticing something about a person in the church or ministry which he or she finds offensive. The antagonist may not even know why they are offended by the person. Factors such as the "dance" or other non-verbal patterns of behavior may cause the person to dislike the soon to be targeted victim. The potential antagonist may be re-creating a parent or caregiver and either expecting more love from the person than is possible or trying to punish the person for being similar to a parent or caregiver. The antagonist may not know why they don't like a person; they just know there is something about the potential victim that they don't like.

Other causes may produce secret antagonism. It is possible that the antagonist may not like the person because he or she is seen as a rival leader who may possibly take the recognition that is wanted by the antagonistic HP. It may be that the antagonist is aware that the target may identify things that the antagonistic HP is doing to harm others in order to gain acceptance. So, the antagonist must make certain that this person is prevented from acting. Or the antagonist

155

may be addicted to proving himself or herself by the ability to rescue a church or ministry. This addiction requires that a new target must be found periodically. In this case, anyone can be a target, but it is frequently someone who may be seen as either a potential or actual rival. Usually, re-creative addictions are at the root of the problem. Regardless of the cause, an attack is likely. Finding a real problem is not necessarily important. Proving to others that the HP is the savior is important. So, the goal is just finding or imagining or creating a problem whether it really exists or not.

The secret phase of the attack then proceeds with secret conversations (see chapters 9 and 14 of *Toxic Church* for more information). The antagonist finds those who are willing to listen to complaints. The receivers of complaints are usually placators, rescuers, victims or martyrs who identify with the HP through the vehicle of re-creation. All of the participants are attempting to re-create the same family dysfunction. A group or "system" slowly forms which mirrors the dysfunctional family group which each individual experienced as a child. These listeners are also looking for acceptance and the antagonist will give acceptance if the enabler will only listen to complaints. This leads to the problem that is described in *Toxic Church* of person A talking to person B about person C. Person C is depersonalized. Person A and B know about person C. Person C does not know what persons A and B know. Person A is the antagonist. Person B becomes the enabler of the antagonist. Person A and B become the first members of what is called a dysfunctional "system" by therapists. The goal is to make person C the "identified patient," the person who is not really the patient, but only is seen by the sick system as the patient. Person C is now the person who is identified as a person who requires correction despite the fact that person C is innocent. Person C is now a scapegoat. In the same way that Adam scapegoated Eve and Cain scapegoated Abel, persons A and B are now ready to scapegoat and attack person C.

The public phase of the attack begins when larger numbers of people are aware of the complaint against the targeted person. The complaints are usually not sin issues. Rather, they are value judgments. Value judgments have the advantage of being able to attract others with the same re-creational needs. In addition, value judgments are not easily refuted because the standard is each individual's personalized belief rather than a clear Biblical boundary. Thus, the complaints are ones like he is preaching too long, she is too structured, he is too compliant, etc. etc. etc. The antagonist and his or her enablers are actually trying to find or create their re-created mothers, fathers or primary caregivers. During the public phase, the person being attacked has little chance of being able to defend himself or herself. If the victim defends himself or herself, others begin to discuss whether there is validity in the attack. This only encourages the attack since success has been achieved in getting others to consider the "sin" of the victim. If the victim fails to make a defense, others state that the problem must be valid since the victim refuses to defend himself or herself. It is assumed that the victim is unable to provide an explanation since the charge has some validity. And remember, the issue that is being discussed is usually not a sin issue. It is a value judgment which can only be evaluated subjectively. Therefore, no reasonable defense is possible as the issue is purely subjective in its evaluation. In any event, whether the victim defends himself or refuses to defend himself, the result is the same. More and more people within the church or ministry are talking about the complaint and wondering if it has validity. In this environment, the target slowly becomes the "identified patient" for more and more people.

The serious phase of an attack takes place when a significant number of individuals have marked the victim as the "identified patient." At this point charges become much more serious as the likelihood that serious charges will be accepted is heightened. They can include ethical charges about the use of money or some moral charge about sexual behavior. The charge can also be an accusation of doctrinal impurity. In fact, many charges concerning doctrinal impurity have nothing to do with real doctrinal problems. Rather, they are rooted in the need of the antagonist to be the savior of the church or ministry by defining what is seen as true doctrinal purity. During the serious phase, it is very difficult for a targeted individual **not** to defend himself or herself. The reason: The charges are likely too serious to ignore. Regardless, the result of defending only confirms the attack. The antagonistic HP has directed attention away from himself or herself and moved it toward the targeted victim. Everyone is talking about the target. No one notices the person who is orchestrating the entire eruption.

And one other important factor needs to be understood during the serious phase. Because the charges are unjust, the victim will normally experience feelings of anger and probable depression. Anger is a normal result of injustice. The victim is being subjected to extreme injustice because he or she is likely being attacked on the basis of the re-created needs of the attacker. This means the target is often being attacked on the basis of things which are completely unknown—such as the victim either not being similar or being similar to the parents or primary caregivers of the troubled person or persons. This injustice will produce anger. And depression may also result as feelings of hopelessness may be present.

The last phase of the attack is the reactive phase. The target is now a true victim. The victim is angry and depressed and will likely react in one of two ways. Either the victim will break out in anger or the victim will leave the ministry. Counselors call this "fight or flight." It is important to note that no matter how functional a person may be, all humans can be pushed so far that these reactions are possible. It is simply a matter of intensity and frequency of attacks over a period of time. So, the victim is doomed. If he or she does not remove himself or herself, anger will result with a probable argument or the rebuke of an attacker. This only dooms the victim. The antagonist and his or her enablers then say, "Look at this behavior. The charges against this person require correction." The person will then be forced to leave or resign. In this situation, the victim may become very depressed and possibly even subject to extreme psychological problems like clinical depression or worse; even suicide can become an alternative for a victim at times. (See *Toxic Church* for further explanation of this possibility).

Chapter 29
Preventatives During the Secret Phase

What does Scripture say about confrontation and how is it to be done? The secret phase of an attack may be the most difficult phase to address as it includes problems that may or may not occur. Since the problem is initially only within the mind of the antagonistic HP and perhaps a few chosen confidants, anyone, other than the antagonist and his or her close friends, has any idea that a potential problem is brewing. It is even possible that the problem may never take place. But those who would prevent or correct conflict must not be disarmed. First Peter 5:8 tells us, "Be of sober spirit; be on the alert. Your adversary the devil prowls like a roaring lion, seeking someone to devour." How can one be alert? First, it is important to know what possible scripts, roles or intensities of roles may be present in the life of the one who might be attacked. Even if scripting is quite minimal, an understanding of these factors is of paramount importance. If a target has placator tendencies, the task of confronting will be much more difficult. Or, if the target has persecutor tendencies, confrontation may be easy, but doing it in a loving and godly manner may not be so easy. A target who is a victim or martyr may never be able to confront. For this reason, it is important for an individual who may be attacked to submit to the exercises which are included in the appendix of this book. These exercises help a potential victim understand what his or her own default reaction is to potential attacks.

It is also important to recognize that attempting to correct those who would cause or allow conflict may provoke an attack (see chapter 13 in *Toxic Church* for more detail concerning this process). In other words, the person who wants to prevent conflict may be the first one to be attacked. The need on the part of the attacker is to prove himself or herself by protecting the church or ministry by attacking a target. The person who would prevent the attempt to protect the church or ministry must therefore be attacked first. Otherwise, the attempt to prove one's self by attacking someone may be prevented.

A very helpful step is understanding the ways that an antagonistic HP can be discovered. As previously discussed, there are several helpful keys to uncover a person who may be willing to attack another in an attempt to elevate the status of himself or herself. A review of these principles is appropriate. Chief among these keys is an examination of the abuse cycle around a person. If there are telltale signs of the presence of the abuse cycle in any part of a person's family, the likelihood of dysfunctional roles being formed in that person's life are elevated. Antagonistic HPs seldom come from highly functional families. This is the reason Paul told Timothy to examine carefully the potential elder's family in 1 Timothy 3:4–5. This means it is important to know the familial background of as many members of a church or ministry as possible. It is particularly important to know the familial background of potential or current leaders. It is my experience that those with difficult family backgrounds or difficult current families often excuse themselves by blaming another member of the family or by saying that their dysfunctional background has had no effect. Do not be deceived by this tactic. Where there is smoke, there is probable fire. Be wary of anyone who has had a very difficult upbringing or has a current family that contains dysfunction. Of course, not everyone who comes from a dysfunctional background becomes dysfunctional, but there is much greater potential for problems having developed in that person's behavior. Be on the alert; be of sober spirit!

Pay close attention to other previously cited ways to identify a potential antagonist. Remember: The identified patient is likely not the antagonist, but the person who does the identifying of a patient is a strong possible antagonist. Note if a person cannot confess a sin. Take special note if a person ever tells a lie. Note who wants to be hero of the organization or ministry. Note who feigns support of a leader, but fails to follow at appropriate times. Pay close attention when a person demonstrates vengeful behavior, but recall that those who are attacked may fall into a reactive pattern of defending themselves in an angry manner. So, discount anger in the lives of those who may have been unfairly attacked. But do note those with vindictive behavior patterns. Note who fails to apply 1 Timothy 5:19–20 and Matthew 18:15–20 when correcting another. And strangely, note those who seem to be a devotee of leadership principles. Ask the question regarding why a person is dedicated to learning how to lead? Is the person trying to win acceptance by gaining more followers?

Another important preventative that should be accepted includes avoiding the "all is well" syndrome. Problems tend to erupt suddenly and without prior expectation. Antagonists wait until the right opportunity appears. So, never hold to the mistaken concept that a church or organization seems to be conflict proof. The silent phase is just that. Silence means that there are no apparent problems. But silence does not guarantee that problems are not festering deep within the heart of some of those within a church or ministry. Be on the alert!

Prayer is also of great importance. A person who is immersed in prayer demonstrates a lack of anxiety and will be seen as a self-defined person. Prayer should also include requests that Matthew 18 can be utilized. Matthew 18 requires in the second step of confrontation that a witness who is willing to confront accompany the primary confronter. Sometimes, finding a witness is very difficult. In addition, finding a witness who is willing to confront may be even more difficult. Before any problem has occurred, in the secret phase of an attack, prayers need to be given to the Lord that if a problem should erupt, witnesses who are willing to confront would surface.

Finally, an important tactic in preventing and correcting conflict that should not be forgotten is the task of developing a team of outside helpers who can assist a pastor, church leader, or any Christian leader if conflict erupts. This is in accordance with Proverbs 11:14 and 12:15. This can be accomplished through a denominational group of pastors or leaders from several churches. Or it can be accomplished through a fellowship of Christian leaders. However it is done, it should be done. An advisory team can be used to help a pastor or leader process a problem when it erupts. The problem of a pastor or leader presenting the principles of this or other books on conflict to his own church or organization is that he will be seen as self-serving.

The principle of Matthew 13:57 states, "A prophet is not without honor except in his own home town and in his own household." In other words, lessons on conflict will likely be better accepted if someone outside of the church or organization presents them to the church or ministry. So, an advisory team member can be asked to teach principles about conflict to a church or organization in order to overcome this problem. And one other thing an advisory team can do during the secret phase is to present the Biblical truths of Matthew 18:15–20 and 1 Timothy 5:19–20 to a church or organization. Once again, if a pastor or leader teaches these things to his own church or ministry, he may be seen as self-serving. Better to have an outside member of an advisory team teach these principles. And there is one other important benefit of an advisory team. If a leader has failed to note a problem in his or her own behavior, members of an advisory team can provide balance and instruction regarding how to address this behavior.

Chapter 30
Steps During the Public Phase

During the public phase of an attack, the real task of how to confront Biblically must be understood. To fail to confront dysfunctional behavior means that potential conflict is being enabled. Recall: When the public phase of an attack begins, the issue that is criticized by an antagonistic HP is often a value judgment. A value judgment is usually based on the re-creative needs of the attacker. The attacker may be trying to win love and acceptance from someone who is a re-created parent or care giver. When the target is not behaving like the attacker's parent or caregiver, that person will be targeted in an attempt to make them behave the way the attacker's parent or caregiver behaved. In addition, the value judgment may be shared by others who are part of the friends and enablers of the antagonist because they have the same re-created needs. The opposite may also be true. The attacker may have found the exact image of the desired parent or caregiver, but the purpose of the attacker is to harm his or her re-created parent or caregiver for a real or perceived offense from the past. Once again, enablers may share the dislike for the target for the same reasons. In either case, charges like these are commonly heard: He is too structured; she is too relaxed; he doesn't feed me when he teaches; she doesn't take care of me; he never visits us; he is so old; she is so young; he dresses like a slob; she dresses like she is an aristocrat; etc. etc. etc. The real charge that is often hidden is that he or she isn't like the father, mother or caregiver that the attacker and his or her enablers are hoping to re-create. Or, he or she is just like the father, mother or caregiver that the attacker wishes to punish for some infraction from the past.

Remember, there is an inherent problem that is revealed if the target attempts to defend himself or herself during an initial attack.

To defend means that the subject of discussion has become the victim's performance or lack of performance. The attacker's behavior remains largely ignored. Therefore, the attacker wins and the victim loses. However, if the victim fails to answer, the result is likely the same. Witnesses of the attack wonder if the reason the victim does not defend himself or herself is because the charge is legitimate and no defense can be made. The final result in either case is that the victim is being seen by more and more as the "identified patient." The victim is not the one doing wrong. But others are giving a great deal of thought to the possibility that the victim is the one doing wrong. The antagonistic HP is allowed to remain, hidden in the background, orchestrating the problem while remaining seemingly innocent.

The public phase of an attack is often begun by what I like to call the "ambush." An ambush takes place when the victim is suddenly confronted without any foreknowledge that an attack is coming. The ambush usually contains what a pastor friend of mine calls "hurtful, but not helpful" statements. It is similar to attempting to bait a person with a trick question or accusation which has the ability to catch a victim off guard. It is kind of a "gotcha" statement. The reason antagonists like to ambush is that they know the victim has had no chance to prepare. There is a likelihood that the victim will react in a manner that can provoke further attacks. For if the victim appears to have lost his or her composure in any way, a finger can then be pointed, suggesting that the victim is either inadequate in some way or is guilty of doing some sin.

Sadly, when the public phase of an attack begins, whether through an ambush or a slowly developing whisper, several certainties must be recognized by the victim. First, when a potential victim is confronted for the first time, steps of Biblical confrontation must begin immediately. A delay of any kind encourages further and perhaps more devastating future attacks. Second, secret conversations have undoubtedly already occurred (Proverbs 26:20). An attacker knows that unless others are regarding the victim as the Identified patient, there is less probability that the attack will be accepted. So, to enlist possible enablers of an attack, the antagonist must resort to secret conversations with potential supporters. Sadly, those who are part of the staff of the victim may also be participants. Staff members may attempt to defend themselves from possible correction from a supervisor by participating in an attack. The person under the authority of a targeted supervisor knows that by diminishing the position of the leader through an attack, correction may be diverted. So, staff members are often involved. In addition, antagonists love to solicit the help of staff members for then the attack seems to gain credibility. Staff members are seen by those outside of the inner workings of an organization as those who are more knowledgeable about the problem.

The way to handle the public phase of an attack is through a principle which I like to call **"zero tolerance."** Zero tolerance is a clear Biblical principle. Matthew 18:15 states, "When your brother sins, go and reprove him in private." Note what Matthew 18 does not say: It does not say reprove your brother after he has sinned 2 times, or 3 times, or 10 times. Biblical confrontation is confrontation which is done the first time it occurs. There is no tolerance in Biblical confrontation. Tolerance is perhaps one of the biggest mistakes which is made in the task of properly applying Biblical confrontation. The easiest time to confront is the first time a sin occurs. The longer a sin is tolerated, the greater chance that confrontation will be more difficult. Why? Because the sinner has learned he can do as he or she pleases. Attacks will likely become much more intense. It is interesting to note that many parents recognize the value of this principle. If children are allowed to misbehave, their behavior doesn't get better; it grows considerably worse. The same is true in any sin situation. The easiest time to confront is immediately!

A preliminary step in the principle of zero tolerance is to evaluate the situation that is presented. A mistake can be made if confronting the sin issue will do more harm than good. As an example, when I was a pastor in the 1980s, I served a church in the southern part of the United States. There was a lady in this church who was very near her one hundredth birthday.

She was born and reared during the Reconstruction period in the South. Reconstruction occurred after the Civil War. It was a time in which many Northerners, who were called "Carpetbaggers," came into the south and financially cheated Southerners whenever they had opportunity. The way Southerners learned to recognize these thieves was that they talked with the northern English dialect of the "Yankee." One Sunday, as I stood at the door and said good bye to people after the worship service, I asked this ninety-nine year old lady how she was doing. She always carried a wooden cane with the brass head of a duck for a handle. She reached up and hit me, gently but firmly with her cane. She said she was doing fine, but would I please stop talking like a Yankee! Now the question was: Should I confront this elderly lady for her lack of love? Of course, the answer is NO! At her age and given the circumstances of her childhood, I needed to be absolutely tolerant of the hit with the duck cane. Incidentally, this lady came back to me the following week with an apology. But the point is that when an attack comes, a preliminary evaluation must be made to determine if the attack should be corrected. Correcting a person may do more damage to the credibility of the victim than the sin can ever do. In a case like the lady with the duck cane, better to allow the attack to remain unchallenged. Her age brought deserved respect from the members of the church. Everyone in the church would understand this lady's attitude and no one would believe her attack was anything more than a relatively minor matter that should be dismissed.

Here is an example of an attack that I did not handle very well while serving as a pastor. It was a dangerous attack that did considerable damage. This issue needed to be confronted. It rose above the level of the duck cane incident. At the end of a worship service, while I was saying goodbye to people at the back door of the worship center, a woman approached me with a request. "Pastor, I want to talk with you." The tone and demeanor in the request clearly betrayed her intent was not friendly. I quickly retreated to a room with this woman to hear her complaint. "Pastor," she said, "You did something very wrong today. You used the word 'stupid' in your sermon and you used it repeatedly. This is not a godly word and I want to ask you never to use it again." I could see fire in her eyes and hear hate in her voice. Then, I did the wrong thing. I said, "Mrs. Smith, I want to ask you to forgive me for using this word. I will do my best never to use it again." She stormed out of the room with a look of satisfaction. Sadly, Mrs. Smith was not done. She came after me repeatedly with other complaints and eventually left the church.

But before she left, she made countless charges about how I was unfit as a pastor. She made very certain that everyone knew she was leaving because I was a very bad pastor who needed to be fired.

How should I have handled this situation? I should have used zero tolerance. Here is how it works: When I heard Mrs. Smith's request to see me, I should have asked her to wait until I had finished saying goodbye to those at the door. To rush to answer her somewhat hostile request rewarded her angry manner. Then, after hearing her complaint, I should have stated something like this: "Mrs. Smith, I am very sorry that I used that word. I am certain that someone probably hurt you by using that word sometime in your past (Remember, she was undoubtedly re-creating). However, there is a problem with your request. There is really nothing in Scripture that forbids the use of that word. In fact, Biblical cognates like the "fool" or the "scoffer" are used quite regularly throughout Scripture, particularly in the Proverbs. In addition, if I am successful in stopping the use of that word, there is the potential that you might find another word in my sermons that you don't like next week and then the week after that. Then, there is the possibility that someone else might find another offensive word. Then, there will be another offensive word and another offensive word and eventually I won't be able to say anything without fearing that someone in the worship service might be offended by something I might say. Eventually, I won't be able to preach at all. Mrs. Smith, I want to make an appeal. The act of using the word "stupid" is not a sin. I'm going to do my best to avoid it because someone likely hurt you with that word sometime in your past. But the act of not tolerating my sermons, devoid of any Biblically forbidden words, is, in fact, a failure to love me. John 13:34–35 tells us that we have a new command to love one another. First Corinthians 13:7 tells us that love bears all things. Mrs. Smith, would you consider praying about this and coming back to me to ask for forgiveness?" I should have then waited a second to see if she was ready to ask for forgiveness. If she defended herself or tried to scapegoat me in another way, I should have repeated my appeal, prayed for her and left the room.

Please consider how this tactic, which I call "**zero tolerance**," serves notice on Mrs. Smith. She knows that the act of confronting her pastor for something that is not a sin issue will not be tolerated.

In no way did I enable her actions by letting her "get away with it." I took immediate action. But something else very important has just happened. I have obeyed Matthew 18:15. Remember: This verse doesn't state that we are to wait for someone to do something wrong twenty or thirty times before acting. It states that when a brother sins, we are to take decisive action at that time. "Zero tolerance" is a Biblical principle. Also, and very importantly, we are then in the position of being able to follow the second step of Matthew 18:15–20 because we have obediently followed the first step of the text which tells us to reprove, in private, a brother or sister when a sinful act becomes apparent.

Something else very important has just happened. Please note how this rebuke is consistent with two other Biblical principles of confrontation. I have attempted to gently correct this woman as 2 Timothy 2:24–26 states, "And the Lord's bondservant must not be quarrelsome, but be kind to all, able to teach, patient when wronged with gentleness correcting those who are in opposition if perhaps God may grant them repentance, leading to the knowledge of the truth, and they may come to their senses and escape from the snare of the devil, having been held captive by him to do his will." Also, in this example, I have appealed to this woman. I did not make a demand. This complies with 1 Timothy 5:1–2: "Do not sharply rebuke an older man, but rather appeal to him as a father; the younger men as brothers, the older women as mothers, and the younger women as sisters, in all purity." I appealed to her by asking her to consider her behavior from a Biblical perspective. This tactic is hard to master. So, I suggest a simple way to learn how to enforce zero tolerance: role play! By regularly role-playing various scenarios, this tactic will become a regular part of a leader's method of handling difficult situations.

In Asia, we have found role playing a very helpful exercise. We have been told that teaching Asians to confront is impossible. However, when we ask students to first role play, and then, as an assignment, go and confront someone who has attacked them, the results are consistently remarkable. One Asian pastor told us the story of a lay leader who publicly criticized him during a church meeting for using the term "Communion" instead of "Lord's

Supper." The attacker told him: We are Baptists. We don't use the term "Communion." We use the term "Lord's Supper." He then publicly made the remark that it was his responsibility to correct this young pastor for his Biblical inaccuracies. We gave this pastor the assignment of correcting this lay leader. We pointed out that the real issue was not "Communion" or "Lord's Supper." The issue was who was running the church! The young pastor came back with a glowing report of what had happened. Though he could not correct the lay leader immediately, as the first opportunity to correct had passed, he could arrange for a meeting as soon as possible. The pastor made an appointment to meet with the lay leader privately. He told the man that the term "Communion" was not forbidden in Scripture. He also told him that the term "Lord's Supper" was not necessarily the only Biblical one. He added that a more accurate term, Biblically-speaking, was Passover. He also pointed out that Jews use the term "Seder" with regularity. He then asked the man to consider his absence of love for his pastor. He cited John 13:34–35 and 1 Corinthians 13:7. He asked the man to pray about the matter and consider returning to him to ask for forgiveness. The pastor did not have to wait. The man immediately asked for forgiveness from his pastor. He also asked the members of the church who heard him correct his pastor to forgive him also. The pastor ecstatically reported to the class that the lay leader, who had continually criticized him, was now one of his most ardent supporters. The pastor added one other thing. He told us that he had begun to use "zero tolerance" with his children whenever he had to discipline them. He told the class that his children were now behaving much better and there was much less conflict within his home.

When zero tolerance is faithfully applied by a potential victim, there are several possible replies which an antagonist may attempt. First, the antagonist may reply with bitter, scapegoating or vengeful statements. When this occurs, the target (who is really not allowing himself or herself to be a victim) should repeat the appeal without deviating even slightly from the appeal. When bitter statements or scapegoating are the response of someone who has been rebuked with zero tolerance, the person has betrayed themselves as a "scoffer or a wicked person" according to Proverbs 9:7–9. A further step after repeating the appeal is to **walk away**. The antagonist is attempting to bring about an angry reply in violation of 2 Timothy 2:24–26. If the potential victim replies in like manner by using angry statements, the antagonist then has ammunition to use in the next step of further attacking the victim. Better to pray and leave the attacker alone by walking away. This confirms the step of zero tolerance. The antagonist has been taught that an attack will not be tolerated when a potential victim walks away from an angry reply to a confrontation.

Even when an angry retort comes from an antagonist after the victim has taken steps of zero tolerance, the potential victim has not lost in the confrontation. The potential victim has clearly identified the antagonist. And, the target knows from whom the next potential attack will occur. Antagonists don't stop attacking when attacks are allowed; rather, they are encouraged to continue with further attacks. So, failing to take the step of zero tolerance has no advantage. But now, when the step of zero tolerance has been taken, the potential victim has drawn a line. The antagonist knows that attacks will not be tolerated. The tactic of slowly destroying the target by slow, steady minor attacks has been eliminated. And enablers of the antagonist are also less likely to participate in further attacks because they soon learn that unwarranted attacks will not be tolerated by the potential victim.

Another possible response on the part of an antagonist is crying or making excuses after having been rebuked through the step of zero tolerance. These tactics are meant to say to the potential victim, "See what you have done to me! How can you hurt me this way?" In this case, the initial appeal should be repeated without the slightest deviation. To deviate from a repeat of the appeal will teach the antagonist that the tactic of tears and excuse making will prevent the target from protecting himself or herself. So, don't let a person get away with excuse making or tears as a reply to zero tolerance. Kindly repeat the appeal and say nothing else.

What if an antagonist actually offers an apology? This too may be a tactic that is meant to disarm a potential victim. For the antagonist can always say, "Well I apologized. What else does this guy (or girl) want?" To prevent this possibility, always ask this question if it is not clearly stated by the antagonist: "Are you asking me for forgiveness?"

If the person can't quite say please forgive me, make an appeal to the person to consider asking for forgiveness and then return for further discussion. If the antagonist balks, cease further discussion. Until the words, "please forgive me," are stated, the antagonist has not reached the point of true contrition. However, if the person can say those very important words, immediately forgive the person verbally and hopefully with a reassuring hug! If the antagonist never reaches the point of true repentance, one of two results is likely. First, the antagonist will take the attack to the serious phase. The other possibility is that the antagonist will leave the church or organization. This is called a "blessed subtraction" and should be welcomed.

There is one other possible response to a confrontation on the part of an antagonist. The antagonist may stay in the church or organization while failing to either apologize or make further accusations against the victim. In that case, all may be well and good. The attacker may be afraid to conduct further attacks due to possible confrontation. However, the potential victim must be wary. Renewed attacks could begin at any time. If new attacks suddenly become evident, the victim has two choices. The victim can either attempt to use the tactic of zero tolerance again or the target may take the steps that are suggested during the next phase of an attack, the serious phase.

One other question needs to be considered. How often should the step of zero tolerance be used? Matthew 18:15–20 seems to describe a single attempt before confrontation with a witness is done. Titus 3:10 suggests no more than two attempts. I would never suggest more than two attempts at using the tactic of zero tolerance. Continued confrontation will likely produce a situation in which arguments may occur. Even if they do not, the attacker has been given further ammunition for he or she can state that the potential victim is belligerent and cannot accept suggestions. When two attempts have brought no success, the next steps of handling an attack with proper confrontation must be considered. The next steps are those which are taken during the serious phase of an attack for the antagonist certainly is considering how future attacks can be conducted.

Chapter 31
Confrontation During the Serious and Reactive Phases

If zero tolerance does not discourage the antagonist, further attacks are certain to follow. The intended victim may repeatedly offend the attacker by means of unconscious and unintended slights or mannerisms which reflect a father, a mother or a caregiver whom the attacker is unknowingly trying to re-create. These offences may produce attacks that are much more serious. The antagonist must "up the ante" so to speak as the initial attacks failed. Thus, in the serious stage charges may be those which are not just value judgments. The attacks will likely include true sin issues. So, charges of theft, immorality or some other heinous sin may be leveled. Charges of doctrinal impurity are quite common during the serious phase. And remember, charges of doctrinal impurity often have nothing to do with the issue of correct theology. They are only an attempt to scapegoat a victim and prove the value of the antagonist. After all, the antagonist is saving the church or organization by ferreting out evil, in this case doctrinal impurity.

At this point, and possibly during the public phase of an attack, the potential victim should have informed his or her advisory team concerning the matter. If an advisory team has not been sought, it is now time to be certain that advisors are found and apprised concerning the situation. One of the reasons that advisors are needed is that the potential victim must become aware of any "blind spots" in behavior that he or she may have. If there is a real sin issue in the life of the potential victim, it must be corrected. An outside team can and should help with this process. Objectivity from such a team is invaluable. It is possible that the problem is not the antagonist's behavior. Rather, the problem may be the behavior of the person who sees himself or herself as the victim. An objective evaluation can help to determine if the issue is a sin issue on the part of the person who sees himself or herself as the intended victim or if it is a sin on the part of the attacker or both.

The next step in the process of handling an antagonist is mentioned in Matthew 18:15–20. The second step is taking one or two witnesses for a second confrontation. The language of the confrontation should not vary from that taken during the private confrontation. However, this step cannot be taken without one or two witnesses. Witnesses must have seen the crime. They cannot merely be those who come along to witness the second confrontation. This presents a dilemma. What if there are no witnesses? Also, what if the witnesses don't want to be involved in a confrontation? If there are no witnesses who are willing to take steps of confrontation, the second step of Matthew 18 cannot be performed. What is the victim to do if there are no witnesses who are willing to accompany a confrontation? First, and most important, the victim must pray that the Lord will provide witnesses who are willing to confront. No further action can be taken until the Lord answers this prayer. However, there is something else the victim can do and it is very powerful. The antagonist will attack repeatedly. The purpose is slowly to wear down the victim and bring the person into reactive behavior. When a victim reacts, the likelihood of unacceptable behavior is much more possible. The antagonist has won in that case. Further charges can be leveled at the victim on the basis of his or her reaction to constant criticism and attacks. There is an alternative that has been suggested previously. It is a very simple step: **Walk Away!** At this point, the potential victim has already obeyed the first step of Matthew 18 on one or two occasions. Further attempts at zero tolerance will have no benefit. The antagonist only wants to provoke a reaction. The attempt is totally thwarted if the victim just walks away from a person who is leveling an attack. If the attacker asks for a private meeting, the intended victim should ask what the meeting concerns. If the answer sounds like another attack, the victim must state that nothing positive will come from another meeting and then just turn and walk away. If the attack comes without a request for a private meeting, the same tactic of turning and walking away must be used.

How long should a potential victim endure ongoing attacks which require the step of turning and walking away? What if the Lord does not provide a witness who is willing to confront? Opinions vary. I believe a victim must begin to entertain the possibility of resignation at this early stage. If a victim's family is being hurt, the victim must regard his or her family first and consider leaving the church or organization (1 Timothy 5:8). I also believe that if a potential victim is coming close to the reactive phase, a resignation should be considered. Each person must decide how much abuse they are willing to endure. Ron Susek, in his book, *Firestorm*, describes a pro-active resignation. This is done after a victim has adequately analyzed a situation, but before he or she has become the identified patient by most within the ministry. When a person resigns at this point, the church or ministry is teachable. They wonder why the person is resigning and they are willing to listen to a loving and clear explanation. The help of an advisory team can be beneficial at this point.

While interviewing pastors for these books, one of the clear mistakes I heard repeatedly was that a pastor stayed too long in an untenable situation. In the US, this may be caused by the cultural value of being the Lone Ranger. The Antidote is a preventative for this problem in the US because the victim no longer attempts to win the acceptance of men by being the Lone Ranger. In Asia, this is caused by the fear of bringing shame to a family or church. The Antidote is also the answer for this dilemma for Asians. Only by applying The Antidote can a victim be freed from the tyranny of shame. Once again, if we have complete acceptance in Jesus, we have no need for the acceptance of men. Shame is an impossibility.

But what if the Lord provides a witness or witnesses who are willing to confront? The same step of confrontation mentioned during the public stage of the attack should be conducted a second time which includes the presence of a witness or witnesses. Only this time, the antagonist is requested to ask for forgiveness from the intended victim and the witnesses, not just to the intended victim. If there is still no apology and a request for forgiveness, or if another attack is mounted, the third step of Matthew 18:15–20 must be conducted. This time the victim and the witnesses must go to the primary decision-making board of the church or ministry. The charges against the antagonist, confirmed by witnesses, should be presented to the board with a request for action according to Matthew 18. Under no circumstance is any kind of a threat toward the board warranted. A victim must never threaten leaving a church or ministry. If the board determines to correct the antagonist, the process is similar to that of the first two steps. Again, the procedure of Matthew 18:15–20 must be followed. The antagonist must be asked to repent and seek the forgiveness of the entire board as well as that of the victim and the witnesses. Something is very important at this juncture: If the board refuses to act, the victim should give serious consideration to a resignation. The reason is simple: The board members, in an attempt to excuse themselves for failing to take proper action, will likely scapegoat the victim. They will say to themselves and others, "Well, we didn't correct Mr. X, but after all Y (the accused victim) was wrong in many ways." Thus, the board is enabling the antagonist and is in danger of allowing homeostasis to become a part of the church or organization (for further information see *Toxic Church*, chapter 10). It is time for the attacked individual to leave the church. Otherwise, the victim will also become an enabler of the evil that is now pervading the church or organization as the victim is allowing himself or herself to be victimized.

Finally, what if the board takes proper action, but the antagonist still does not repent? The fourth step of Matthew 18 must be taken. The matter must be brought to the entire church or organization. Once again, no threat is ever to be issued toward the organization or church by the victim. And once again, if the organization fails to act, resignation must be considered because the organization or church is headed into homeostasis through the action of scapegoating the victim.

What if this process fails at any point? The matter is quite simple. The victim must consider resignation and/or leaving the church or organization. As cited in *Toxic Church*, chapter 18, resignation at the right time is of key importance. To leave too early causes a victim to lose perspective as he or she does not fully understand the situation. To leave too late, after the victim has been labeled the identified patient by most within the organization, means that the person has lost all credibility. Thus, statements of protest or explanation will not be considered as valid. Leaving before the point in which the victim has been labeled the identified patient by a significant majority leads to a marvelous teachable moment within the church or organization. Many will be shocked by the resignation. They will ask the victim why he or she is leaving. The victim should then explain without any animosity or personal protestations. Names of attackers and specific details do not need to be mentioned. The likelihood is that many will hear and believe what has happened. Correction of the church or Christian ministry is then much more likely.

If an attack goes uncorrected or if a victim stays too long in a dysfunctional organization, there is high likelihood that the victim will become reactive. He or she will likely develop severe depression or problems with inappropriately expressed anger or both. When members of the church or ministry see a depressed leader or one who is subject to inappropriately expressed anger, the likelihood of a forced resignation or firing is very high. The church or ministry has failed to protect the victim. Rather than assume responsibility for the emotional condition of the victim, the members of the ministry or church will scapegoat the victim. The leader will be dismissed while everyone within the organization justifies themselves by repeating the unjust charges against the leader. The point is simple: If you are a victim who is not finding relief from the attacks of an antagonist, leave the organization before you become reactive. You will not prevail if you find yourself constantly attacked with no opportunity to prevent the attacks! The antagonist will eventually win and you will be forced to leave, either by your own emotional collapse or due to a forced resignation or firing!

Things to Remember about Biblical Confrontation

1. Remember the importance of prayer throughout each stage of confrontation.

2. Confront an antagonist as soon as the sin issue is known—immediately if possible! **"Zero Tolerance"** Matthew 18:15; Luke 17:3

3. Confront as gently as possible—scripting means the person confronted doesn't know what he or she is doing and may be

unknowingly under the control of the Devil—2 Timothy 2:24–26

4. Make certain the confrontation is in the form of an appeal—1 Timothy 5:1–2

5. Confront alone, without a witness, no more than two times—Matthew 18:15; Titus 3:10

6. Don't defend yourself when confronting if the confrontation is received with a rebuke, anger or an attempt to scapegoat. This response confirms you are talking to a scoffer or a wicked man and you should not continue with the confrontation. Instead, simply **"Walk Away"**—Proverbs 9:7–9

7. Reject someone confronted unsuccessfully two times and remove the person from any leadership position if possible—Titus 3:10

8. If the initial confrontation is not successful, continue with the steps of Matthew 18:15–20 if possible.

9. If attacks or hostile words continue and you are unable to apply the follow-up steps from Matthew 18:15–20 use the principle of **"Walking Away."**

10. If attacks or hostile words continue and you are unable to apply the follow-up steps from Matthew 18:15–20 or if your family is being hurt, strongly consider resignation—1 Timothy 5:8

Chapter 32
Protect or Correct? How to Really Help a Leader

There are other ways to hurt a pastor, church leader, or Christian organizational leader. One of the ways is by failing to take simple Biblical measures to correct or to confront the attacker of a leader. Since it is very difficult for a victim to defend against an unjust attack, if you are a witness to an attack, you are in a much better position to correct the attacker. As a witness you should confront the attacker according to Matthew 18:15–20. If it becomes necessary to resort to the second step of Matthew 18, a second witness is already available in the person who was the object of the attack. By protecting a pastor or a leader in the early phases of an attack, you may prevent a great deal of conflict in your church or ministry.

Should a pastor or leader ever be confronted? Of course! If a pastor or leader has committed a sin, they must be confronted. It is amazing to me how often I hear of Christian leaders who become immersed in some sin pattern. And when I do, I always wonder where the other Christians were who were supposed to confront that person before he or she became involved in sin.

There is an important Biblical limit when confronting a Christian leader. The only sin which can be confronted is a sin which is clearly defined by Scripture as being a sin. Any other possible offense is off limits. If an issue is confronted which is not a clear, Biblically-defined sin, there is strong likelihood that the real issue is prompted by an unmet re-creational need on the part of the confronter. I am aware of a Christian group that teaches that if a male leader wears a red tie, he is going to hell. He also leads others to hell by his example. So, this group confronts their leaders for this and many other dress code violations. The problem is this particular sin is not a Biblically defined sin. It is an offense that has been created by a hero-persecutor who must validate his or her own life by saving a church in some ridiculous way. There is no limit to the need for these re-creative eruptions on the part of an antagonist due to the process of addiction. So eventually an antagonist or an antagonist and his or her enablers get around to declaring red ties and many other silly things a sin. In this situation, not only can a person be rebuked for dress codes, but also for mannerisms, speech patterns and all types of imagined sins. What the antagonist is really doing is trying to make himself or herself into the hero of the ministry by protecting others from supposed crimes. Never ever confront a Christian leader for a sin that is not clearly defined as a sin in Scripture. Period!

If the process of confrontation of a pastor or elder becomes necessary, 1 Timothy 5:19–20 must be obeyed. This passage requires a special manner of handling the confrontation of an elder which is somewhat different from that of Matthew 18:15–20. First, this passage requires that the discussion of the sin issue of an elder cannot be entertained unless there are two or three witnesses. This means if you hear an accusation against an elder by only one person, you must confront the complaining person because they have not obeyed 1 Timothy 5:19–20. The person must be corrected in the same manner that has been previously described with the use of Matthew 18:15–20: zero tolerance, etc. In addition, since this passage is directed at Timothy, it infers that only an elder, like Timothy, can hear the charges against an elder. An elder has the ability to correct another elder. Speaking only to an elder about a matter prevents gossip about a matter. In addition, this passage requires that those elders who continue in sin must be rebuked in the presence of all. This suggests that the offending elder has had a chance to correct the sin. But, if the elder, after being corrected, continues in sin, there is no second and third step as there is in Matthew 18. The elder is corrected in the presence of all. This passage is very important for a couple of reasons. First, the elder is protected from frivolous charges that are not witnessed by at least two witnesses. However, the church or ministry is also protected because the sin actions of the elder are dealt with very firmly. By strictly following 1 Timothy 5:19–20, an elder can be either protected or corrected properly.

But how do we correct for practices that do not glorify the Lord, practices that do not necessarily fit into a category of sin? Or, how do we correct for performance issues within the staff of a church or Christian ministry? These matters are in the hands of those whom God has ordained as the primary decision makers of a church or Christian ministry. Scripturally, the term elder applies to senior decision-making board members. The elders of a church or ministry have the responsibility of correcting if some practice is not glorifying the Lord. As an example, what do you do if your pastor or leader is unskilled in the task of being a personal evangelist? Nothing! Unless, of course, you are on the board which is ordained by the Lord to help correct should this problem exist. In this situation, the board of a local church or ministry should provide training for someone who needs further training and provide measures of accountability to be certain the leader is being faithful in the task of making disciples by sharing the gospel. However, there is one important caveat in the matter of correcting someone for a performance issue. Elders must also be Biblically qualified to serve in these positions. It is important to note that those who do not work in the ministry of the Word do not have the authority to correct those who do! Elders are those who do the work of the ministry of the Word (see 1 Timothy 3:1–7; 5:17–21; and Titus 1:5–9).

In what other ways can a pastor or leader be protected? First, purpose never, ever to entertain a critical thought about a leader. In fact, criticizing a leader for a non-Biblical sin requires asking for forgiveness from the Lord. If the complaint reaches the ears of others, they must also be asked for forgiveness. Remember, it is likely that critical thoughts are the result of un-met re-creational needs. The sin lies in the mind of the critical individual, not in the actions of the leader. Second, we must only correct a pastor or leader with the strict observance of 1 Timothy 5:19–20. Observing this passage in the correction of a pastor or elder helps to protect that leader from accusations that are based in the unmet re-creational needs of antagonists.

What do you do if you just don't agree with a pastor or leader and there is no Biblical sin that the leader has committed? The answer is simple: love the leader! Remember your concern may be rooted in your own re-created needs. So, apply the principles of Romans 12:19–21. Purpose to be that person's champion. The benefits of this step are numerous. First, your attitude toward that person will change remarkably. In addition, you will win that person's heart. As Paul said in Romans 12:21, "Do not be overcome with evil; but overcome evil with good." Once the relationship with the person who offends you is one of love and respect, you have an opportunity to do something that might not occur without the application of this principle. You may have the opportunity to give advice concerning the matter that concerns you. You may also have the opportunity to give advice about other matters. There is nothing wrong with giving advice. It can be quite helpful at times. However, it is almost guaranteed that your advice will not be heeded without a bond of love between you and the person who receives your advice. But if love is present, it is much more likely that the person will heed your advice and the problem may be solved.

I remember an occasion when the staff member of a church came to us with a complaint about the senior pastor of his church. He listed numerous ways in which the senior pastor was inept and offensive. The senior pastor seemed to be a very disagreeable person according to this description. We first asked the question as to whether the senior pastor had sinned in any way. Though there were numerous offences, the answer was "no." There was no real sin to report. So, we suggested that the staff member go through our lessons on understanding the effects of the abuse cycle on himself. We also refused to hear further charges against the senior pastor; thus insuring that we were obeying 1 Timothy 5:19–20. Finally, we suggested he apply Romans 12:19–21 to his relationship with his senior pastor. The staff member accepted our counsel. The results were remarkable. After studying the abuse cycle, the staff member reported that he realized he was trying to re-create his own father through the senior pastor. He hadn't liked his own father and the senior pastor was similar to his father in many ways. He also reported that as a result of applying Romans 12, a relationship of love had blossomed whereas previously there was only dislike between the two of them. There are many ways to protect a pastor or a leader. Perhaps the first way is to protect himself or herself from you!

One other issue should be addressed before leaving the subject of protecting or correcting any member of a church or ministry staff. There is a problem which unfortunately is a reality in many churches and Christian ministries. The problem is sloth. There are those in ministry who are not faithful in the performance of their work. When senior board members of churches or ministries, the elders, are not active in the ministry of the Word, enabling this problem is much more likely. A board member who does not participate in the ministry of the Word is unlikely to correct a pastor or leader for the same failure. Oftentimes, the excuse is used that a person is faithful, but the Lord has not chosen to bless in some way. While it is important to acknowledge that the Lord is the One who produces the growth in our ministries (1 Corinthians 3:6–9), faithfulness, which includes abiding in the Lord, will normally produce results (John 15). Stating that faithfulness has been maintained when it has not is truly a sin. A person who is slothful is likely a person who was not corrected by parents or others either in childhood or as adults for being unfaithful in their work. Sadly, we have personally seen instances of laziness within the ranks of ministry. In one case, we knew of a man who was the pastor of a church in a large city that had less than twenty people for a period of over twenty years. He never did anything, to our knowledge, to faithfully share the gospel with anyone. He just preached on Sunday and was a nurse maid for his twenty people. The church had a large bank account which he constantly drew upon for his salary. When the church was out of money, he retired and the church closed its doors. In another case, we knew of a man who was the pastor of a city church that never exceeded 50 people for a period of 20 years. Once again, this man never made any attempt to share the gospel or do anything that might help the church grow. This church also closed its doors. And sadly, I have had, on two occasions, very unfaithful associates who were totally willing to let me do their job as well as my own. In both cases, resolution of the problem was extremely difficult. (I have also had many very faithful associates who continue to do well in ministry).

The Lord does not honor sloth. Matthew 25:14–30 contains a simple story about three slaves. Two were faithful and were given a differing number of talents according to their ability by their master.

Both had an increase. The master commended the two though the increase was different for each slave. In each case the master stated, "Well done good and faithful slave." However, one slave was not faithful. The lazy slave did not handle his talent faithfully. The result was a strong rebuke from the master. The master said to him, "You wicked, lazy slave… Therefore, take away the talent from him, and give it to the one who has ten talents…. And cast out the worthless slave into the outer darkness; in that place there shall be weeping and gnashing of teeth." Other verses also demonstrate the necessity of faithfulness in work such as Matthew 7:7–8; 28:19–20; 2 Thessalonians 3:10, etc. etc. etc. And Solomon clearly understood that work was not a punishment; it was a reward (Ecclesiastes 5:18).

These verses suggest one thing: Slothful ministry leaders, whether paid or unpaid, need to be confronted and rebuked if they are unfaithful. Unfaithfulness in ministry occurs in many ways. Perhaps one of the most serious is disobedience in obeying the Great Commission of Matthew 28:19–20. Of course, the procedures of Matthew 18:15–20 and 1 Timothy 5:19–20 need to be followed with those who are not faithful in the work of ministry of the Word. But failure to be faithful in the Lord's work is a very serious matter. And those who do not confront lazy ministry workers are enablers of their laziness.

Small group sessions should be ongoing. At this point, exercise 3 should have been completed and The Antidote should have been identified as the result of the initial questions of exercise 4.

Part 5
The Antidote and Discipleship

"Go, and make disciples…"
Matthew 28:19–20

Chapter 33
The Nature of Discipleship

"If you were of the world, the world would love its own, but because you are not of the world, but I chose you out of the world, therefore the world hates you." John 15:19

The interrelationship between The Antidote and discipleship is quite apparent throughout Scripture. In the process of discipleship, a disciple learns to value himself or herself on the basis of the love of God. This is contrary to the values of the world as humans naturally attempt to find value through the acceptance of men. Consequently, the world rejects the disciple, viewing the behavior of the disciple as strange and unnatural. The result of the discipleship process is a progressive alienation between the disciple and the world as the disciple grows more to value the love of Jesus and ceases to value the acceptance of men.

This natural antagonism between the values of the world and values of a true disciple of Jesus is evidenced in many ways. Consider this central lesson that every disciple must learn. Disciples are "fishers of men" according to Matthew 4:19, Acts 1:8, etc. Sharing the gospel and being a fisher of men is one of the most intimidating tasks a Christian can face. The reason is simple. Christians know that they can do many spiritual things without the risk of being rejected by men. Going to church, reading the Bible, prayer, and most other spiritual disciplines seldom risk rejection by those who are not Christians. However, the instant a Christian begins to vocally share the gospel, everything changes. Vocally sharing the gospel always risks being ridiculed and ostracized by non-Christians (and sometimes by Christians as well). If a Christian has not rejected gaining the acceptance of men, sharing the gospel and being a "fisher of men" is extremely difficult. Fear of the reaction of men will likely dominate the feelings of any Christian witness who has not learned to forsake the acceptance of men. This means the application of the principle of The Antidote, either through a formal course or through a long-term discipleship process, becomes necessary if a Christian is to become a true disciple and a fisher of men.

In addition, this natural antagonism between the world and the Christian disciple is manifested in many other ways. Consider these verses:

> The world cannot hate you, but it hates Me, because I testify of it, that its deeds are evil. John 7:7

> If anyone comes to Me, and does not hate his own father and mother and wife and children and brothers and sisters, yes, and even his own life, he cannot be My disciple. Whoever does not carry his own cross, and come after Me cannot be My disciple. Luke 14:26–27

> And as they were going along the road, someone said to Him, 'I will follow you wherever you go.' And Jesus said to him, 'The foxes have holes, and the birds of the air have nests, but the Son of Man has nowhere to lay His head.' And He said to another, Follow Me.' But he said, 'Permit me first to go and bury my father.' But He said to him, 'Allow the dead to bury their own dead, but as for you, go and proclaim everywhere the Kingdom of God.' And another also said, 'I will follow You, Lord; but first permit to say good-bye to those at home.' But Jesus said to him, 'No one, after putting his hand to the plow and looking back, is fit for the Kingdom of God.' Luke 9:57–62

> Go therefore and make disciples of all the nations, baptizing them in the name of the Father and the Son and the Holy Spirit, teaching them to observe all that I commanded you; and lo, I am with you always, even to the end of the age. Matthew 28:19–20

The point is: A disciple learns to forsake the love and acceptance of every aspect of the order of this world and become satisfied, totally and completely, in the love and acceptance of Jesus. When a Christian is immersed in the love of Jesus, true contentment and fulfillment is possible. Without experiencing this contentment in Jesus, the Christian continues to struggle, as do those in the world, in an attempt to find contentment on the basis of the acceptance of men. Contentment based on the acceptance of men is impossible. It is only an illusion. The contentment the world offers cannot be attained because the process is an addictive one without any potential to find complete fulfillment. When the principle of The Antidote is taught, formally or informally, as a part of a discipleship program, the process of learning to find contentment in Jesus is learned.

Discipleship was not a new concept in Jesus' time. It had been an establishment throughout the ancient world, but particularly in Greece and Israel, the only two countries that were known for widespread freedom of speech. A disciple was a man who followed his teacher everywhere for a period, not of days, or weeks, or months, but for years. The task of the disciple was to soak up everything from the disciple maker: behavior, teachings, experiences, practice, etc. Then, the disciple was to take those same concepts and teach others in the same way that he or she had been taught. We have an example of this pattern in ancient Greece: Socrates mentored Plato; who mentored Aristotle; who mentored Alexander the Great. This was also a common practice in Israel. We are told that Paul had sat at the feet of Gamaliel (Acts 22:3). This meant he lived with and learned everything from Gamaliel for a period of years. This was exactly the same method that Jesus used in the training of The Twelve. We see clear evidence of the process as the disciples literally spent over three years in a training program with Jesus. What they were taught is listed in the textbooks which we call the Gospels. These books are the training manuals we are to continue to use today. Jesus taught the disciples about loving each other. He taught them about prayer. He taught them about the Word. He taught them about personal holiness. He demonstrated evangelism and He sent them out on missionary journeys. He taught them about the Cross. Through these lessons, Jesus taught the disciples the principle of being content in His love. In addition, The Twelve were not alone in the process. We have indication that their families were likely with them. Luke 8:1–3 mentions that there were women with the group of disciples. Paul complained in 1 Corinthians 9:5 that he had the right to bring along a wife as did Peter and the others. These same lessons can be learned through the teaching of The Antidote through a Biblical discipleship program.

The lessons learned through discipleship produced significant results. Acts 17:6 tells us that Christians in the first century world were "turning the world upside down." But how did they accomplish this task in such a relatively short period of time? Of course, the Holy Spirit was empowering the early Church. But, there were also other considerations which help us understand how the Church grew so rapidly. Consider the Apostle Paul. We think of Paul as being a gifted preacher, teacher and scholar. But the Biblical evidence presents a somewhat different picture. As an example, in Acts 20:9 we see that Paul's preaching put a man to sleep. The man fell out of a window and died! The Lord did heal the man, but what do we learn from this story? Paul's preaching may have lacked any serious ability to keep his audience interested. In fact, this passage makes us wonder if he was any kind of a spell binder at all! However, other accounts of Paul demonstrate similar problems with his teaching style. In 1 Corinthians 2:1–5 Paul confesses that in his teaching he did not have superior wisdom or speech. He also told the Corinthians that he came to them in much fear and trembling. Finally, Paul added that he had no persuasive words which he could use to convince the Corinthians. These verses portray a picture of Paul that is not particularly complementary. Paul describes himself as trembling and fearful. He also says that he doesn't know what he is talking about and even if he did understand the concepts he wanted to convey, he had no skillful way to present the message. In 2 Corinthians 10:10 it gets worse. Paul quotes his antagonists when they say that though Paul's letters are quite intellectual, his appearance is unimpressive and his speech is contemptible! "Contemptible" as the New American Standard puts it! That's quite an indictment. So, we learn that Paul, the great Apostle to the gentiles (Acts 9:15), was not a spell binder in speech and his appearance was not impressive. And he wasn't a skillful speaker. He even killed a man with his preaching. So, how did he become a primary catalyst of the words, "turning the world upside down?" Only one clue is given in Scripture beside the dramatic help of the Holy Spirit. Wherever Paul went he was always training someone else. He always obeyed the principle of discipleship. He was a true disciple maker. And as he taught his disciples, he also demonstrated many of the same lessons that are taught through The Antidote. Paul said, "I have been crucified with Christ; and it is no longer I who live, but Christ lives in me; and the life which I now live in the flesh, I live by faith in the Son of God, who loved me, and delivered Himself up for me" (Galatians 2:20).

When Jesus gave us the Great Commission of Matthew 28:18–20, He told us to: "Go and make disciples." He did not tell us to go and make Christians. In fact, the word Christian is only used two times in all of Scripture. And, He did not tell us to go and make believers for Scripture only uses this word three times. He told us to: "Go and make disciples." The word "disciple" is used 269 times in Scripture. That was what Paul was doing. He was making disciples. And this was what Jesus commanded us to do. Paul wasn't a spell binder, but he was obedient to the Great Commission. That's all it took! And, that gives hope to you and me because you and I don't have to be spell binders. We just have to be obedient. That's something we can do. We can't control whether we are spell binding preachers, but we can control our obedience. What a relief! And with the help of the application of The Antidote within a Biblical discipleship program, becoming an effective disciple, including learning how to accept being rejected by men, is quite doable.

Disciple making is critical and, with rare exception, the type of disciple making that Jesus did is practiced very little today. Often, disciple making is seen as participating in hearing a weekly sermon or in a regular Bible study. This is not what Jesus had in mind as we examine the gospels. Discipleship was a 24-7 practice of learning and experiencing lessons from Jesus. I would also go so far as to say that making disciples should be the primary means of building any church or Christian ministry today. Here's why: If I were to disciple just three men for the next three years, and then they do the same and so forth, the world is completely reached in slightly over 100 years! Do the math. It works out! This is what Paul taught when he stated in 2 Timothy 2:2, "The things you have heard from me in the presence of many witnesses, these entrust to faithful men who will teach others also." Do you see the four levels of discipleship that Paul describes? Paul teaches Timothy, who teaches others, who teach others. This was how disciple making was and is to be the primary method of church planting and church growth.

Why isn't discipleship a more prominent part of Christian ministries? Very seldom is discipleship a strong part of the ministry of the local church. And often it is very seldom a strong part of other Christian ministries. Even Bible colleges and seminaries often place little emphasis on discipleship. Discipleship might be the most important and possibly the most overlooked principle in all of the Bible! Confrontation is critical because it is a necessary Biblical method to stop those who bring conflict into any church or ministry. But discipleship not only prevents bad behavior, it promotes good behavior. A disciple learns that gaining the acceptance of men through the use of a harmful script or role must be forsaken. A disciple learns that by contentment in the love of Jesus, problems caused by harmful scripts cease.

Why is discipleship not an integral part of every Christian ministry? Because becoming a true disciple means losing the acceptance of men. Often, Christians fear this dramatic step. They have not yet learned that true contentment can only be found in learning how to live in the fact that Jesus has already given us all the acceptance and love we will ever need. When the disciples first followed Jesus, they learned to forsake the acceptance of men and live in His acceptance through three years of intensive training which included leaving homes and businesses (Matthew 4:18–22). The key to disciple making today requires some method of helping Christians overcome the fear of losing the acceptance of men and learning how to live in the love and acceptance of Jesus. One of the ways this can be done is by teaching The Antidote.

But once The Antidote is used in the task of developing healthy disciples, other benefits are also possible…

Chapter 34
Followship

This principle literally jumped off the pages of Scripture when I found myself in a puzzle about why I was confronted with conflict in a local church ministry. Way back, when I was beginning to dabble in ministry, my mentor challenged me to covenant with God to give time each day to Scripture memory. I accepted the challenge and made a vow to God in which I would dedicate a certain number of minutes to Scripture memory every day. The vow included that if I missed a day or two, I would make up the lost time the following day. When I began to memorize parts of Joshua 1, I was enthralled by what I was memorizing. In Joshua 1:7–8 we see that God promises success and prosperity to the man or woman who is strong and courageous and spends daily time in meditating on Scripture. Joshua 1 also says that every place upon which a man or woman's foot would tread would be his or hers (1:3). And it also states that no man would stand against that man or woman (1:5).

It is now more than 46 years later. And guess what? It didn't work. I have kept the vow, but I have not seen the success that these verses promise. In fact, I can state without reservation that I have seen men stand against me. I can go further to state that on a couple of occasions I was greatly harmed by opponents. These painful events were contrary to what I had learned in Joshua 1:5 and all of Joshua 1. Why did this happen? As I pondered, I noticed something: I am not the only one who found failure despite what these verses seem to promise. I realized that Moses, the predecessor of Joshua, did not succeed whereas Joshua did. Moses failed to lead the people into the Promised Land. Joshua succeeded. Why? I pondered these verses and noticed that they require a man must be strong and courageous and immersed in the Word. So, I thought, perhaps Moses didn't know the Word. Ridiculous! He wrote the Word contained in the first five books of the Bible (these five books were all that had been written in the time of Joshua). I pondered that perhaps Moses was not strong and courageous. Also ridiculous! Just reading the story of Moses and Pharaoh in the book of Exodus demonstrates Moses was very strong and courageous. So, what was the difference between Joshua and Moses? And, what was the difference between Joshua and me?

Then, I noticed something else about Joshua. He was a man who, in obedience to the command to be strong and courageous, told the people some remarkable things. He told them that they were to prepare for crossing the Jordan. And he gave them a timetable of only three days. Would they listen to him when Moses had just died and they had spent forty years wandering around without entering the Promised Land? Then, he picked on the Reubenites, the Gadites, and the half tribe of Manasseh. He told them they were to leave their children, their wives and the livestock behind in the land beyond the Jordan (what we call the country of Jordan today). Then, they were to cross the Jordan River before their brothers. Literally they would be the first to cross the Jordan into what we today call Israel. They would be first in and last out should retreat be necessary. This meant that their wives, children and livestock would be unprotected. Joshua required this of the two and a half tribes on the basis of a commitment they had made to Moses earlier. But realize what this meant to these people. Israel had been plagued with the Amalekites as they journeyed toward the Promised Land. The Amalekites made a practice of raiding the stragglers, stealing, murdering and kidnapping as they attacked. In addition, two kings of the Amorites, Sihon and Og, had just been defeated by Israel. The Amorites lived in the region of what was called "Beyond the Jordan". They were a group of militaristic, warlike people who invaded the Middle East, flooding over the Caucus mountains from the north beginning about 2200 B.C. By the time of Joshua, they had been in the land the people of Israel were invading for approximately 800 years. They were called Caucasians because they crossed the Caucus Mountains. They were known for being fierce fighters who were also taller and stronger than the other people of the Middle East (they were also known for being white skinned, blue eyed and intellectually inferior). The

Amorites were far from done with opposition to Israel. Why should they submit to these newcomers in the Middle East? The Amorites would be a thorn in the side of Israel throughout the pages of the Old Testament. The Amorites, as an act of retribution, were certainly likely to attack the undefended wives, children, and livestock, left behind in the land of Jordan by the two and half tribes. If the Amorites didn't attack the stragglers of the Reubenites, the Gadites and the half tribe of Manassah, the Amalekites certainly might. This meant that Joshua's command to these tribes was extremely challenging. We might even say it was rather foolish. But this challenge showed that he was truly strong and courageous. There was a strong likelihood that they would resist. Why would anyone accept such a foolish challenge? Why would anyone allow his wife, his children, and his livestock to be placed in such danger?

Then, I realized why Joshua was successful and why Moses was not. As I considered the story of Moses, I remembered that Numbers 13–14 presented a different story about Moses. The people had refused to obey Moses when he urged them to go into the Promised Land. But notice the response of the people to Joshua in Joshua 1:16–18! Verse eighteen may be the most important words of the Old Testament for had they not been stated; the nation of Israel might never have come to exist. The people, including the Reubenites, the Gadites and the half tribe of Manassah, answered Joshua with these words: "Anyone who rebels against your command and does not obey your words in all that you command him, will be put to death." Then, they added, "Only be strong and courageous." Three times God told Joshua to be strong and courageous in Joshua 1:1–9. Joshua was given the same command from Moses twice in the book of Deuteronomy. Likely the reason Joshua heard these words so often was because he needed to hear them. He likely had a fear problem. But, the people said the same words, "be strong and courageous." It suddenly occurred to me why Joshua succeeded while Moses failed. The issue was not Moses or Joshua's understanding of the Word or their being strong and courageous. They both knew the Word and both were strong and courageous. Though Joshua had to be encouraged to be strong and courageous, he certainly demonstrated strength and courage in the commands he gave to the people in Joshua 1. The issue was the response of the people, not the knowledge or strength of the leader! Moses failed because the people failed, not because he himself had failed. The people would not follow Moses. And Joshua succeeded not because he had succeeded, but because the people succeeded when they chose to follow him.

This means something very simple which is often misunderstood. We believe that if we apply good leadership principles, we will succeed. There is nothing wrong with studying leadership principles. But Scripture teaches something else that must also be understood. Leaders are not in control of their success. Their followers are! Simply put: Leaders don't make leaders; followers make leaders! Let me put it another way: Jesus did not call us to be leaders; He called us to be followers. Is this not what He said in Matthew 4:19 when He said, "Follow Me and I will make you fishers of men?" Due to our own cultural influences and self-centered thoughts, we believe we are in control of our destinies through leadership principles. We are not! Leadership principles can help us, but nothing changes the fact that followers are actually the ones who are in control. Being strong and courageous and also studying the Word of God is very important. But followers have something of a trump card when it comes to making a leader successful. If they choose not to follow the leader, failure is likely. But if they choose to follow the leader who is ordained by God, and faithful to the Word of God, and strong and courageous, success is certain. When a leader fails in life, it may be the followers who are at fault. This is a freeing thought for those of us who have tasted failure. Another simple way of putting this is something I learned as a pastor. No matter how well placed my attempts to cast a vision for a congregation were, I always learned there was always, always, always someone on the back row of the church (or the front row) who could say with certainty, "Pastor, you can't make me!" That person was right. I had no power to make anyone do anything unless the Lord motivated the person who was opposed to my ministry to change and follow my leadership.

This principle is contained throughout Scripture. The book of Ephesians contains a marvelous picture of the relationship between a husband and wife in chapter five. We learn in this chapter that a husband is commanded to love his wife, but he is not commanded to lead her. (Check it out: Ephesians 5 simply does not command a man to lead his wife. In fact, the command to lead a wife does not exist anywhere in Scripture.) The only way a husband can become the leader of the home is if his wife chooses to submit to him. In this way, a wife is actually the one who is in control of the direction of the marriage. In like manner Jesus spoke of the same principle in Matthew 20:24–28 when He described how leaders are not to force those in their charge to do anything. He said that forcing others was the way gentiles acted. His disciples were not to do so. Rather, they were to submit themselves to those in their charge, those who were below them in position! Once again, they were to place their followers in control. This is the same principle that is contained in Joshua 1 where we learn that the followers are actually in control. This picture mandates the leadership pattern of any church or ministry. Christian leaders don't lead the way the world suggests. Christian leaders lead, but they don't control the reaction of the followers. And church and ministry leaders can't lead until followers follow and not before. So, church leaders can use any leadership principle that they may choose, but when they understand that the follower has the last word, then and only then, is Biblical servant leadership affected within the church or Christian ministry.

How does this principle fit into the principle of discipleship and how is this related to the principle of The Antidote? Through the principle of The Antidote, men learn not to value themselves because men accept them, but because Jesus accepts them. This means they can also become disciples because part of being a disciple is learning to disregard the acceptance of men and follow Jesus. When men become disciples, they learn to follow Jesus and accept the rejection of men. This was the command Jesus gave to the disciples in Matthew 4:19 and John 21:19. And Joshua teaches that, when men become followers, leaders can lead. And when those ordained by God are allowed to lead, well you get it—nations are born (like Israel) and the victories of God are seen. So, The Antidote, properly applied through a truly Biblical discipleship program, allows men to become true followers of Jesus. And true followers allow leaders to succeed. But there are still more benefits from The Antidote and the process of discipleship....

Chapter 35
An Abundance of Counselors

Something else can also happen when disciples are taught to follow. When I was a student leader within a para-church Christian organization, I had opportunity to see something which changed my life and lives of those whom I was discipling. I was in graduate school and a graduate resident advisor in a fraternity house (a glorified housemother). The man who was mentoring me from the para-church organization led me to start a fraternity Bible study. Several men joined the Bible study and a couple of them became Christians. Then, my mentor asked me to take these men to watch me witness to students in a nearby dormitory. I was absolutely panic stricken. I had never done any witnessing in that manner! But I felt I had to follow my mentor. So, I took two of these men with me to witness in the nearby dormitory. We prayed in the foyer of the dormitory and then started knocking on doors. I really had very little idea what I was going to say or what I was going to do if someone happened to answer a door. I was petrified with fear! At the first door, no one answered. I felt great relief. Then, we successively knocked on about another eight or nine doors and no one answered. I felt greater relief! Then I told the fellows who were with me that it was likely that the Lord didn't want us to do any witnessing on that day, but just in case, we should try one more door. We knocked on one more door and I was terrorized to see the door start to open. A giant of a man opened the door. He was as tall and as wide as the door opening. I started fumbling for words and somehow said that we were from a Bible study and wondered if he had any interest. I was certain he would say NO and I would be off the hook. But he opened the door and pointed to his desk. On the desk was an open Bible. He said he had been wondering about the Bible and asked if we would explain it to him. He explained that we were in the athletic dormitory for the university football team. He was the only one in his room because all the other men were eating at an unusual time due to their training schedule. He said the only reason he wasn't with them is that he had been wondering about God and decided to stay in his room to read his Bible. As I began to talk, I noticed that the Lord was giving me the strength and the words to speak. All of us sensed the presence of the Lord in the room. Before I could finish sharing, he asked if he could invite Jesus Christ into his heart. This man became a Christian on that day and we later learned that he went to seminary and became a pastor! What a miracle. We had seen God at work. But what is important to note is this happened because I had determined to follow my para-church mentor. And even more important is that the two men who decided to follow me saw God at work. They experienced Matthew 28:20: "And lo, I am with you always, even unto the end of the age." Both of these men became active evangelists throughout the fraternity house. One of them was a Jewish man who had found his Messiah! And I soon left graduate school and began my first steps into full time ministry.

Scripture teaches a simple principle. We all have a need for counseling. Proverbs 11:14 teaches, "Where there is no guidance, the people fall. But, with an abundance of counselors, there is victory." In addition, Proverbs 12:15 teaches, "The way of a fool is right in his own eyes. But a wise man is he who listens to counsel." There are many things a group of counselors can do to help someone in ministry that they cannot do themselves. Every Christian leader has the potential of becoming ensnared in a default script or role. A group of godly counselors can assist in the task of preventing this from occurring. Godly counselors can also help a Christian leader with any sin issues that may exist in his or her life. A group of Christian counselors can help to identify a potential antagonist or help to analyze the history of the church or ministry which may suggest that conflict is possible. The members of a godly group of counselors can help to confront antagonists. The members of a group of godly counselors can teach things to the members of a church or ministry which the leader may not be able to teach without seeming self-serving. And when a leader is under attack, godly counselors can help the leader understand when he or she is becoming reactive and whether or not the leader should resign.

It is also important to understand that there are reasons that we fail to avail ourselves of the benefits of good counselors. Westerners and particularly Americans are often affected by a particular cultural factor. Don't forget: We Americans often see ourselves as the Lone Ranger! The Lone Ranger doesn't need help. He succeeds on his own. Consequently, we don't think we need help from others! To seek the help of others seems like a weakness to us. However, not just Americans have this tendency. Asians may fail to seek counsel because of Confucian ideas which teach that leadership should never be challenged. Therefore, in an Asian cultural context, a leader seeking the counsel of others on a ministry team may find the members of the team reluctant or even resistant to giving advice to a leader. Thus, advice is not sought. But, regardless of the reason why, Westerners and Asians all tend to tell themselves: We don't need any help! We are so smart, so competent that we have the solutions for all of our problems. Sure, we pray and we depend on the Lord (or so we tell ourselves); but the reality is that we will not take help when we are confronted by problems because we think we already have all of the answers that we need. We say to ourselves that we only need the Lord to empower the answers we already have. In addition, leaders often don't want anyone taking away their recognition by solving problems that they face in their ministry. This happens because in the likeness of Adam, leaders may believe their value and acceptance comes from the recognition of men. And if a leader seeks the help of another, he or she is somehow risking the ability to perform in some way and thus lessening his or her importance in the eyes of men.

Participation in the act of making disciples and being a disciple through the process of The Antidote corrects the tendency to disregard offering or accepting advice. The real reason we don't accept advice is that we believe we lose the acceptance of men if we don't have all of the answers for every problem. The application of The Antidote in our lives causes us no longer to fear losing the acceptance of men by accepting advice. In addition, the reason we don't give advice is due to the fact that we fear that someone may not accept our advice and we may consequently lose that person's acceptance. Once again, The

Antidote corrects this error. We can offer advice without concern for whether or not men accept our advice. Our acceptance is not based on whether men accept or do not accept our advice; it is based on the acceptance of Jesus. Thus, the sharing and accepting of advice is not a problem for the disciple who has learned the principle of The Antidote.

This sharing and accepting of advice leads to a great benefit. The disciple learns from the advice of the disciple maker. But as the result of a willingness to accept the advice of the disciple maker, the disciple eventually understands all of the truths which the disciple maker offers. A disciple becomes like his disciple maker. As Jesus said, "A pupil is not above his teacher. But everyone, after he has been fully trained, will be like his teacher" (Luke 6:40).

When a Christian becomes a true disciple, he begins to follow the one who is discipling him. In the same way that the two young men saw God at work when we shared the gospel with the football player, the disciple learns that by following, he or she can see the blessing of God. The disciple also learns that the acceptance of men is no longer needed and that in the acceptance of Jesus, complete fulfillment is possible. This was why the two young men became faithful witnesses for Jesus. Joshua 1 teaches that faithful followers allow their leaders to become strong leaders. But as the followers follow their leaders, something else happens: The followers also become leaders. The miracle of Luke 6:40 occurs. In other words, great followers have the potential to become great leaders! And great leaders can form a group of counselors who have the potential of forming a highly effective ministry team. This ministry team may then provide an abundance of counselors which lead to victory according to Proverbs 11:14 and 12:15.

But, there is still another benefit that comes from the application of The Antidote....

Chapter 36
Discipleship and the Polity of the Church or Ministry

As disciples become followers and followers become leaders, these highly trained and effective leaders can then become elders, deacons and primary decision makers throughout the ministries to which they have been called. One of my colleagues puts it very well. "When we become disciple-makers, we stop harvesting leaders; we start mentoring them!" What a simple concept. And how important it is. When someone comes into a church who is a successful professional of some kind, we often see church and other ministries make the same mistake: They enlist these people as ministry leaders when everything in Scripture clearly indicates that a leader must be tried over a period of time, not days, not weeks, not months, but years (1 Timothy 5:22). In addition, ministry leaders must be faithful ministers of the Word (1 Timothy 3:2b; Titus 1:9). But we often place those into leadership who have little or no experience in the ministry of the Word. The example of Jesus was that He trained His disciples over three years. Why do we resort to a standard which is dramatically different? When we harvest rather than disciple, we invariably find leadership teams filled with those who have problem scripts and roles which will potentially, given enough time, result in conflict.

The discipling of key leaders in any church or ministry is not a new concept and where it is used, significant growth is evidenced. When I was a student leader within the para-church organization, I saw how it was that those within the para-church ministry lost their fear of men and lived in the love and acceptance of Jesus by a simple method. Within five weeks of the conversion of an individual who was being discipled through that organization, the new Christian was taught how to be a personal witness and was asked to participate in witnessing. One of the greatest pastors I have ever known was Richard Jackson. He was the pastor of North Phoenix Baptist Church, one of the largest churches in the city of Phoenix and one of the largest churches within his denomination. Pastor Jackson required his church leaders to visit and witness every week. If they could not or would not do this, they could not become or remain leaders within his church.

The key to the health of a local church or ministry is the health of the leadership of the organization. Please refer to and read *Toxic Church*, chapter seventeen for a Biblical description of the organization or polity of the local church. The reason these Biblical qualifications for church leadership are contained in Scripture is to emphasize the necessity of training ministry leaders. The Biblical way that leaders were trained was through the vehicle of discipleship. Extreme care is evident in the pages of the New Testament in the choice that Jesus made in Luke 6 of the original disciples. He also constantly trained them in techniques of ministry (note Matthew 10, Luke 9–10 and countless other portions of the Gospels). As noted in Scripture, elders were not just decision makers. They were those who did ministry and were highly scrutinized for the office (1 Timothy 3:1–8; Titus 1:5–9). The first elders were disciples. In other words, the vehicle of discipleship was the best way to develop godly leaders who could lead Christian ministry in New Testament times and it is the best way to do so today. Thus, discipleship is a key to developing healthy church and ministry team structures which are able to prevent conflict from erupting. And one of the ways to prepare leaders for true discipleship is through the application of The Antidote in their lives within a discipleship program. For an example of a pastor who was able to change a church through the process of discipleship, see *Toxic Church*, chapter 19.

But, there is still one other benefit of The Antidote within a discipleship program. And this one has the potential to dramatically change the atmosphere of any local church or ministry....

Chapter 37
Discipleship and the Culture of the Ministry

The Antidote has another benefit which should not be overlooked. Love hunger does something strange to each one of us. We constantly yearn for acceptance. In order to find those who will give us acceptance, we tend to seek those who appear more likely to favor us with acceptance. We naturally classify these people into groups according to dress, speech, occupation, educational level, possessions, etc. We also look for non-verbals like the "dance" and any other way we can find those who we believe will give us acceptance. We can also unconsciously or consciously reject those we believe are unlikely to give us acceptance. So, a person who speaks, acts or looks unfamiliar in any conscious or unconscious way can be rejected. In fact, the tendency to group ourselves among those whom we think will give us acceptance are what causes cultures or subcultures to develop. These factors mean that because we seek the company of those who we believe will give us acceptance, we tend to congregate with certain people. These forces may cause a church or ministry to develop its own unique subculture which distinguishes it from any other church or group of people. Every local church or ministry may have its own distinct subculture which may be clearly recognizable in some ways and not so recognizable in other ways. The final result is that each church or ministry can manifest its own unique language patterns, dress, etc. Educational levels, occupations and other factors can produce harmony or division, uniting or dividing a church or ministry accordingly. (For further information, see: Creech, Christopher P., *The Relevance of Selected Cross-Cultural Principles of Communication in Preaching to Subcultures.* Ph.D. diss., Southwestern Baptist Theological Seminary, 1992).

If cultural differences between individuals within a church or ministry and visitors who happen to come to that church or ministry are significant, the visitors may be rejected. The fear that the visitor with cultural differences will not offer acceptance to others within the church causes this rejection. And in dysfunctional churches or ministries with highly scripted members, this can produce attacks on those who are believed to be unlikely to give acceptance to the controlling group within the church or ministry. Unless a new person demonstrates an immediate willingness to comply with any whim of a hero persecutor or the enablers of the hero persecutor, that person will be rejected. This may occur for reasons that are not recognized due to the fact that the cultural characteristics of the visitor may not be consciously evident. If a number of people come into a ministry setting with their own cultural distinctions and their own hero-persecutor and enablers, and another group within the church or ministry has their own cultural distinctions and their own hero persecutor and enablers, the potential for a split is quite high.

Subtle ways this problem occurs are quite common. A new pastor at a rural church was accustomed to visiting with people around the pulpit after a worship service. His culture taught him that those who wanted to ask questions about his sermon would best do so at a relatively private place around the pulpit. However, the church had a non-verbal custom in which the pastor always stood at the entry door of the church to talk to those who had questions. Several of the members of the church believed he didn't want to talk to them after the church service because he did not wait to talk to people at the entry door of the church. They assumed he would only talk to a favored group who approached him near the pulpit. His ministry only lasted a few months. A pastor at a church in the South might be complemented with the words, "Pastor, you did a good job today. My toes are very sore (meaning you stepped on my toes)." However, to use the same methods of preaching in many other areas of the US would be rejected. People would feel as if they were being scolded and unloved. The pastor would experience a short-term pastorate.

There are important ways that a pastor or any ministry leader can navigate around these problems. First, and very important, recognize that every church or ministry has a distinct culture and if you are not a part of every aspect of that culture, you don't know the rules. In addition, the members of the church or ministry don't know that you don't know the rules. They may assume that your unconscious, counter cultural behavior is motivated by an attempt to reject the majority culture of the church or ministry. Second, always be willing to change your own culture to fit the culture of those within your ministry. But, never violate Scripture to do so. Third, if the cultural differences are too great between you as a leader and the members of the church or ministry, consider not attempting to work within that ministry. There may be too many potential pitfalls and chances are, as the new leader, you will eventually be rejected. It is also possible that you will unconsciously or consciously reject the members of the church or ministry. The result of either eventuality is disaster. The new leader will either be accepted or rejected because of cultural differences that may be unrecognizable to both the leader and the members of the church or ministry.

An important part of any strategy which attempts to mitigate these factors involves a careful study of the culture of any church or ministry. To do this, there is a very special "Secret Weapon." If a leader will carefully disciple a member of the congregation or ministry team who is completely immersed in the culture of a church or ministry, the disciple can be asked about the unwritten rules, values and desires of those within the ministry. This is a particularly helpful technique if the person who is being discipled also understands the culture of the pastor or leader. In this case, the disciple will likely have greater insight into where potential violations of the culture of the church or ministry may occur. Still greater advantage is found if the disciple is a cultural leader within the church or ministry. In this case, his or her acceptance of the new leader will become apparent. The members of the church or ministry will then likely overlook cultural mistakes. After all, they say to themselves, if good old Tom (or Dick or Harry) likes him, he must be OK!

But there is a solution which will eliminate these problems entirely. If a discipleship program is instituted in which the principle of The Antidote is taught, Christians slowly learn how to cease valuing themselves on the basis of the acceptance of men. They will no longer congregate into groups in which it is hoped they will find acceptance while rejecting members of other groups where they unconsciously feel they will not gain acceptance. The reason: Each Christian knows the acceptance of Jesus is sufficient and the absence of acceptance from anyone within the local church or ministry is unimportant. In other words, with the proper application of the principle of The Antidote, cultural divisions will cease. No longer will men need to segregate themselves into groups where it is believed they can find acceptance. Why? They already know they have all the acceptance they will ever need from Jesus. And with an elimination of cultural divisions, based on a need to gain the acceptance of men, many of the causes of conflict and strife will also cease to affect a church or local ministry.

There is another benefit of the application of The Antidote which is a game changer. Church and ministry groups often tout their own friendliness. And usually they are very friendly with those who are a part of their own cultural circle. But unknowingly they may reject others who are not a part of their cultural circle. To others they may seem anything but friendly! Why: People naturally congregate with those whom they believe will give them acceptance. And, they naturally shun those whom they believe will not give them acceptance. In other words, people naturally and unknowingly accept or reject others on the basis of whether or not it is believed that acceptance can be found within a particular group of people. Thus, to some people a church or ministry may seem very friendly because they are part of the cultural group of the church. But to others, the church or ministry is a very unfriendly place and one to be avoided. Why? These other individuals do not appear to be a part of the majority cultural group of the church. Thus, they are judged as unlikely to return any love and acceptance which is given to them. So, love and acceptance are either consciously or unconsciously not offered to them. To these people, the church is very unfriendly.

But if the members of a church or ministry no longer seek or need the acceptance of men, they are free to offer acceptance to anyone, even to those whom they believe will not return their acceptance. Why? They no longer need the acceptance of men. This means they no longer tend to accept some and shun others. The result is that a church or ministry truly becomes a place where friendship and love are offered to all. In this situation a church becomes a magnet for all people for one simple reason: All people are looking for love! And if a church offers love, without any consideration for whether or not a visitor has the capacity to return love, that church will find that people literally "beat down the doors" to get in. This ability to disregard the need for human acceptance is a benefit of The Antidote. This means that when the principle of The Antidote is widely taught within any church or ministry, the love that is produced will prove to be a significant force for the growth of that ministry.

Small group sessions should be continuing. Plans for the implementation of steps from exercise 4 should now be in process. With exercise 4, the potential for long-term application of the principle of The Antidote is the goal.

Chapter 38
R.B., *The Antidote* and Discipleship

Remember R. B? He was right! Wildwood Church had a real problem. Something had to be done. The surface issue was that Wildwood was in slow decline. But, R. B. handled the problem the wrong way. R. B. scapegoated the pastor. But the pastor was not the only problem. The entire church, including R. B., was at fault. As the members of the board at Wildwood are analyzed, a clear picture emerges. The three members who left the church after Pastor Harry had been fired had likely been involved in enabling a system within the church which was bringing about its slow death. They saw no need for change. Their failure to realize there was a significant problem stopped them from acting before R. B. finally resorted to drastic action. R. B. and his son, Bryan, also had a significant problem which caused them to handle the problem badly. As young men, both had attempted to win acceptance and validate themselves through athletics. When athletics no longer served the function of winning acceptance, they resorted to a new addiction: ministry! R. B. tried to validate himself by saving the church (hero) through the act of tackling (persecuting) the problem pastor. Bryan tried to save the church (hero) by beginning new ministries for younger families who might potentially become a part of the church. Joe, the codependent friend of Bryan, was an enabling rescuer who wished to help Bryan validate himself though ministry. Bryan and Joe enabled R. B. as rescuers and placators when the scheme to fire the pastor surfaced. The other two remaining board members were also placators who went along with the scheme to remove the pastor even though they had significant reservations about such a dramatic step.

What was really going on was there were dysfunctional scripts, running rampant throughout the board of the church and throughout the entire church. The older church members weren't innocent. They had allowed a dysfunctional system which was killing the church to persist. They were more interested in their own comfort by having a caring pastor and worship services which catered to their own likes rather than address the church's need to survive. And don't forget Pastor Harry. Harry too was likely too selfish to change the church. He had a comfortable situation in which he could coast into retirement. Thus, he became the primary placator of a dysfunctional and selfish church which cared little for the survival of the church or for the growth of the Kingdom of God. In other words, the entire system within Wildwood was wrong. R. B. was just as guilty as the other members of the church who had disregarded Matthew 28:19–20. No one was sharing the gospel except Bryan. And Bryan was obeying the Great Commission without the permission or encouragement of the church. As is always the case, the problem wasn't Pastor Harry or R. B. The problem was a church wide system of dysfunction, including numerous scripts which predetermined that a split would eventually occur.

What was the answer? Only with an effective method of discipleship, engaging a significant part of the church, would dysfunctional scripts be identified and eliminated. This discipleship would necessarily include steps to repent of finding acceptance for one's self on the basis of human recognition and instead base acceptance only on Jesus' love. In other words, The Antidote needed to be applied to leaders and members of Wildwood through an effective discipleship program.

R. B. could have been the pivotal leader who could redirect the church without scapegoating the pastor. A simple plan, involving R. B., requires that he had to first become a disciple and then a disciple maker. He had to apply The Antidote to his own life so that he could lose his fear of losing the acceptance of men. As a consequence, he could also become a faithful personal witness for Jesus. In addition, fear of offending others by asking them to share the gospel could also be eliminated through the use of The Antidote in R. B.'s life. In this way, R. B. could become a true disciple maker throughout the entire church. As more and more disciples were made throughout the church, pressure would mount on the leadership to become disciples and disciple makers as well. The pastor would also be affected. Eventually, Wildwood Church could become a dramatically different place, alive, vibrant and a church that was obedient to God's call for this special church.

Chapter 39
Strategies that Work!

We live in very troubled times. The powers of the abuse cycle and the Fall are wreaking havoc throughout almost every culture. Each successive generation is experiencing greater and greater levels of love hunger. The result is that more and more seek to find those who promise to offer acceptance while shunning those who may not. This is causing large scale, increasing divisions between cultures and subcultures. In addition, there is an increasing need for love hungry people to find someone who can be re-created to fill the void of love that is left by a missing or dysfunctional father or mother. This means that antagonism toward leaders and by leaders is also growing quite dramatically.

This antagonism is extending itself into Christian ministry circles as well. The discipline of conflict resolution has dramatically grown in the last few decades to address this growing problem. But the problem continues to grow. As I have been teaching these principles, I have found a significant number of Christians who are strong advocates of the principles contained in this book. Particularly supportive are those who have experienced the pain that comes when they have found themselves attacked by those who claim to be Christians. In addition, a significant number of advocates are evident among leaders who realize the problem cannot be solved only by traditional conflict resolution practices. This is particularly true among Asian leaders, but it is also true among many Western leaders.

However, the material that you have just read contains concepts which are somewhat foreign to many within Christian leadership circles. Most conflict resolution programs assume the possibility of redirecting the lives of those who are either antagonists or the enablers of antagonists. This attempt may prove powerless due to the power of the addictive scripts of those who enable conflict. This material suggests a different approach. Rather than attempt to reason with those who enable conflict, this approach suggests assuming that many dysfunctional individuals are held captive by the Devil and cannot be convinced that what they are doing is wrong. In this case, the only solution is that the Lord intervenes in the lives of the dysfunctional in some way and grants them repentance (2 Timothy 2:24–26). In other words, individual Christians are often powerless to deal with the problems presented by those who are the cause of conflict. This means that rather than attempt to coerce dysfunctional individuals to change, the task is one of learning how to work around dysfunctional individuals. The primary step that is suggested is to confront these individuals. The secondary step, should confrontation fail, is either to remove the dysfunctional individual from the power structures of Christian organizations or to remove the potential victim from within the organization. If these actions are not taken, the net effect is that those who attempt to intervene as well as the victim have become enablers of the antagonist.

I have found myself somewhat puzzled by the reality that some Christian leaders are opposed to the concepts presented in this book. However, I believe I understand why this is occurring. Many within Christian ministry circles are addicted to finding the acceptance of men on the basis of their own ability to solve problems within any ministry. This may be one of the factors that causes leaders to seek to become leaders. In other words, they are addicted to winning the approval of men by saving an organization from the destructive forces of conflict. The program that is suggested in this book requires that the Christian admit failure in some situations and learn to disarm the power of those who promote conflict by working around them. Those who are addicted to being heroes are reluctant to accept the fact that they may fail in efforts to prevent conflict. These leaders may also refuse to consider a program or a teacher who they fear might threaten their hero status. The result is that they may encounter failure in conflict resolution by unwittingly enabling those who promote conflict. However, when Christian leaders accept the reality that some cannot be coerced to behave functionally and determining to accept that reality, the result may be success where other methods have failed. That success comes when leaders teach how to avoid dysfunctional problems by confronting or disarming those who promote conflict.

I am dedicated to one reality in my own life. I must never attempt to gain acceptance on the basis of my own ministry. In other words, my value must come from the love of Jesus and not due to the acceptance or rejection of this material. In other words, I am committed to the principle of The Antidote in my own life on a daily basis.

But I am left with one strong belief. The principle of The Antidote, consisting of learning to value ourselves on the basis of the love of Jesus, can dramatically reduce the problem of conflict and pain within Christian ministry. Toward this end, I ask each of you to prayerfully consider how you might be a participant in the teaching and use of this material. My prayer is that by reading The Antidote and applying the principle of The Antidote, your ministry and understanding of the problem of conflict can produce a significant decline in this problem.

A new commandment I give to you, that you love one another, even as I have loved you, that you also love one another. By this all men will know you are my disciples, if you have love for one another. John 13:34–35

This ends the lectures of the course. The remaining task is to complete a significant portion of the exercises assigned during the small group sessions. The facilitator should lead the members of the small group through at least exercise 4, step 3 before ending the course. The remaining steps of exercise 4 should be completed over time with either the continued meetings of the small group, a good accountability partner or a trained Christian counselor.

The Antidote

Appendix

Small Group Instructions
Confidentiality Statement
Exercises
Local Church Survey

The documents can be reprinted with permission from the author.
Please make copies for your small group dicussions.

Small Group Exercises

The following pages contain the small group exercises that have been suggested as a tool to be used at various points throughout the lectures. These exercises are designed to help each student apply The Antidote in his or her life. Once, having made this application, steps can then be taken which prevent the destruction that can come from dysfunctional scripts which result from attempting to gain the acceptance of men.

There are some important directions that need to be mentioned again concerning these exercises. First, it is very important that the statement of confidentiality, which is included with these exercises, be enforced rigorously. Every participant should be required to sign this statement, including the facilitator. In addition, a signed copy of each person's confidentiality statement should be given to each participant. The importance of confidentiality cannot be overstated. It is my experience that when confidentiality is ensured, the small group discussions are very helpful for each participant. Without the assurance of confidentiality, it is unlikely that the small group exercises will have the beneficial effect that is intended. It is also important that each point of the confidentiality statement be emphasized to each participant.

There should be no more than four and no less than three participants in each small group plus a facilitator. The reason for this limited number of participants is quite simple. Fewer than three participants and a facilitator make meaningful interactions somewhat difficult. More than four participants and a facilitator make the task of answering the questions within the exercises quite laborious for the entire group. In other words, the process becomes too slow with more than four participants and a facilitator.

The procedure for the exercises is quite simple. First, a time of prayer within the group should be conducted in which the Lord is asked to help each person share and observe each of the parts of the confidentiality agreement. This prayer should begin each session and each session should also end in prayer.

Then, each person should be asked to verbally answer the questions of each part of each exercise. As an example, each person should answer exercise one, question one before proceeding to exercise one, question two. After exercise one is completed, the same procedure should be followed for exercise two, and then exercise three, and finally, exercise four. While a person is answering, the facilitator should record as much as possible of how each person answers the questions. Separate pages should be kept on legal pads or a notebook for each person. A computer should not be used in the small group sessions. Electronic media, by their very nature, suggest that confidentiality may not be a priority. In addition, the presence of a computer can provide a distraction. But if the facilitator merely writes down the answers on a pad, distraction is limited. It is also important to note that at the end of the course, each person's written answers must be returned to that person with an assurance that no copies have been made. In other words, no written record of the answers is left with anyone other than the participant who gave those particular answers. Thus, confidentiality is demonstrated as a priority.

The purpose of recording the answers of the individual participant is to provide help in analyzing his or her answers in the completion of exercises three and four. As the facilitator writes down the participant's answers, he or she should underline any repeated statements and any statements which betray emotion. Statements which demonstrate the emotions of gladness, sadness, anger or fear should be underlined (mad, glad, sad or afraid). Then, before the participant begins exercise three, his recorded answers should be repeated for everyone in the group to hear. As the answers are repeated by the facilitator for the entire group, underlined repeated statements and underlined statements of emotion should be mentioned. The purpose is not only that the participant hears a second time what he or she has said, but also others within the group also hear again what the person has said. In this manner, the likelihood of analyzing the participant's possible scripts by both the participant and other members of the group is significantly increased. Exercise three provides opportunity for each member to contribute to helping each person analyze his or her scripting possibilities.

The purpose of the small group is to help each person complete the exercises up to exercise four, question three. Exercise four, questions four and following, need to be completed over time with the help of others. Plans for the continuation of the process of completing exercise four should be considered for each person within the small group before closing the final session of the small group meetings.

Confidentiality Statement

BEFORE PROCEEDING WITH THE EXERCISES OF THIS CLASS, EACH PARTICIPANT IS REQUIRED TO SIGN THIS PLEDGE. IF A PARTICIPANT IS UNABLE TO SIGN THIS PLEDGE, THAT PERSON IS RESPECTFULLY ASKED TO DISMISS HIMSELF OR HERSELF FROM THESE SMALL GROUP DISCUSSIONS IN WHICH OTHERS ARE OPENLY SHARING ABOUT THEIR PERSONAL LIVES.

As a participant in this class, I covenant to keep these promises:

1. Never to share, under any condition, anything that is said by another participant in these exercises with anyone unless I have express (written) permission from the members of the small group in which the comment was made, and particularly from the person who shared the comment.

2. To share as openly and honestly as possible about my own life, ministry, and relationships.

3. To encourage others to share as openly and honestly as possible about their own lives, ministries, and relationships.

4. Not to dominate discussion, allowing others to have adequate time to share their stories as I also have adequate time to share my own story.

5. To make suggestions with each member of the group regarding possible scripts and help to identify The Antidote for each person's life.

6. To accept and evaluate the statements of others regarding my own possible scripts and possible suggestions in the identification of The Antidote for my life.

Printed Name:_____

Signature: _____

Date:_____

Exercises

EXERCISE #1

TEN WAYS TO KNOW IF YOU ARE IN NEED OF DISCUSSION ABOUT YOUR HEALTH IN MINISTRY AND TO IDENTIFY THE ANTIDOTE FOR THE SOLUTION OF MANY OF YOUR OWN LIFE AND MINISTRY PROBLEMS:

1. Are you driven by any compulsions? (Some of these may be good compulsions, caring for others or working hard)

2. Are you bound to the ways things were done in your family of origin? (What are the voices of the past-from childhood?)

3. Do you demonstrate maturity in your relationships with others? (Do you have difficulty confronting others? Do you think others must change in order to fit your own needs?)

4. Do you believe your happiness hinges on the behavior of others? (Do you think if you find someone, something or some event, everything will be alright?)

5. Do you feel inordinately responsible for others? (Did you take care of others in the past? Do you feel the need to care for others now?)

6. Do you vacillate between dependence and independence in your dealings with others? (Do you frequently find yourself angry at others-the same ones whom you feel responsible for their welfare?)

Appendix

7. Do you find yourself denying the problems evident in your family of origin? (Do you feel your father or mother was perfect and therefore there were no problems in your family of origin?)

8. Do you worry about things you cannot change? (Do you try to make people who are close to you healthy even though you have no real power to change them?)

9. Are your emotions punctuated by extremes? (Do you find yourself vacillating between extreme love for someone who needs your help followed by dislike because the person either fails to improve himself or herself or improves too quickly?)

10. Are you looking for something missing inside? (Do you have a sense of deep inner vacuum, a sense that there must be more in life?)

Appendix

EXERCISE #2

THE ABUSE CYCLE: ANSWER EACH OF THESE QUESTIONS IN
THE HEARING OF THE MEMBERS OF YOUR SMALL GROUP
WITH THE HOPE OF GAINING FURTHER INSIGHT INTO THE
ANTIDOTE FOR YOUR LIFE.

1.   Is there any love hunger in your life? Did you receive enough nurture
     and love as a child? (Did you have two parents in the home? Were your
     father or mother physically or emotionally absent during much of
     your childhood? Did you have enough money as a child? Were your
     parents overly strict or indulgent? Did they discipline inconsistently?
     Did either of your parents have any sort of an addiction problem?
     Were you subjected to any verbal, sexual or physical abuse as a child?
     Did either of your parents expect you to care for them when you were
     a child? Do your parents expect you to care for them now? Did either
     of your parents expect you to do things that they were good at doing?
     Did either of your parents expect you to behave as others in the family
     behaved? Did either of your parents ever ridicule you? Did either of
     your parents scold you too often?

2.   Was there any magical thinking present in your life as a child? (What
     did you do to please your father or your mother? Did you find yourself
     doing these things repetitively? What was the result?)

3. Were you ever depressed as a child? (Were you ever treated for depression as a child? Did you have any attention deficit problems as a child? Did you have any behavioral problems as a child? Did you have any problems with eating either too much or too little as a child? Do you ever remember being sad as a child? Did you ever feel as if Dad or Mom didn't like you? Can you remember any event in which Dad or Mom was disappointed with your performance in any particular area? Were you accepted or rejected by your peers?)

4. Has there been any attempt at re-creation in your life as an adult? (Have you seen any physical or behavioral similarities between the important people in your life as an adult and those of your parents or primary caregivers? Have you seen any repetitive patterns of relational problems in your life as an adult? Do you have difficulty dealing with authority? Do you find yourself drawn to certain people for no apparent reason? Are you bitter when certain people seem to either disregard your presence or reject you? Do you see a connection between the people you crave as friends as an adult and your own parents or primary caregivers?)

5. Do you frequently experience depression as an adult? (Are you being treated for depression? Are you anxious about things that you cannot control? Do you fear rejection, particularly from certain individuals? Do you feel sad? Are you lethargic? Would others describe you as a depressed person? Do you ever have thoughts of hopelessness? Have you ever contemplated suicide? Are you aware of being depressed and the feeling that the depression will never go away? Do you have any sleep problems?)

6. Do you have any addictions or dependencies? (Are you controlled by any behavioral patterns such as anger, anxiety, depression, critical spirit or gossip? Do have any addictions to money such as saving, spending or gambling? Are you a compulsive over-eater or under-eater? Do you work over sixty hours per week? Do you care for people emotionally, physically or spiritually whom God has not placed in your care? Do you feel guilty when someone around you does not take your advice? Do you feel slighted when someone disregards your advice? Do you give advice to people when they have not asked for it and God has not made you responsible for their welfare? Do you have problems with immorality? Do you have problems with drugs or alcohol? Do you have a need to have perfect order in certain areas of your life? When was the last time you asked someone within your family to forgive you for anything? When was the last time you asked someone outside of your family to forgive you anything? Do you have difficulty confessing to others? Do you find yourself angry at one person or another frequently?)

7. Are you giving your own children inadequate love? (If you have children, do you see the same patterns and problems in your own children's lives that were in your life? Are you children living happy, fulfilled Christian lives? Do you feel guilt for the failures you are seeing in the lives of your children? Is this guilt justified? What should you do about it?)

Appendix

EXERCISE # 3

PLEASE COMPLETE THIS EXERCISE AND PRESENT YOUR
ANSWERS DURING THE APPROPRIATE SMALL GROUP
DISCUSSION TIME. THESE ANSWERS SHOULD HELP IDENTIFY
THE ANTIDOTE WHICH CAN SOLVE MANY OF THE PROBLEMS
YOU HAVE OR MAY SEE IN YOUR LIFE AND MINISTRY:

Which of these roles were evident in your childhood?

1. HERO- The hero is the child who does everything necessary to
    keep the order of the family intact. This is the child who may clean
    the house, mow the lawn, shovel the snow, take care of the smaller
    children, do the laundry or care for a physically or emotionally ill
    parent.

2. SCAPEGOAT- The scapegoat is the black sheep of the family. This is
    the child who always takes the blame for the problems in the family.
    This child may be the one who is unfairly accused by siblings and
    unfairly punished by parents.

3. MASCOT- The mascot is the child who can dissolve every stressful
    situation with a laugh. This child is a master of giving the most
    ridiculous response or smile at the right moment.

4. LOST CHILD- The lost child does everything necessary to remain
    unnoticed. When family conflict or tension arises, this child attempts
    to become a part of the woodwork.

Were any of the following intensities of the above roles a part of your life
as a child? These roles tend to enable various addictions and dependencies.

1. PLACATOR- The placator will do anything to satisfy the protests of an
    upset member of the family.

2. MARTYR- The martyr will pay any personal price to keep peace in
    the family. The martyr will always assume responsibility for a problem,
    even if not responsible for that problem.

3. RESCUER- The rescuer will do anything to salvage a situation. They
    will even excuse family dysfunctions. As an example, the rescuer will

always excuse Daddy's physical or sexual abuse by saying that Daddy has had a bad life and should be understood.

4. PERSECUTOR- The persecutor is a master of blaming everyone for a family problem. However, they will never blame themselves. The spirit of Adam is clearly a part of their character. They are unpleasant people to be around and almost impossible to appease.

5. VICTIM- The victim accepts the persecution of the persecutor. This person may not be the real victim. The real victim often does not see himself or herself as the victim.

Ask your colleagues to estimate which of these roles and intensities of roles may be evident in your life?

If your colleagues are correct, what are the implications for your life and ministry?

Now, after listening to the comments of your colleagues, answer the same questions about yourself a second time. Which of the roles and intensities of roles do you think are a part of your life? Have they been a part of the magic thinking process in your life? Have they been a part of re-creation in your life as an adult?

Recognizing the importance of 1 John 1:9 is very critical at this point! What you have identified as a sin issue to confess is The Antidote which will help you gain insight and help for many of the problems you have already encountered or will encounter in your life and ministry. How do you gain the acceptance of men? What script is manifested in this attempt? What is your Antidote?

It is the responsibility of each small group member to direct and possibly correct each individual small group member concerning items of confession that may need to be applied to each small group member's life.

What are the implications for your life and ministry?

Are you properly suited for your present ministry assignment? Is it possible that a re-assignment is needed?

Appendix

EXERCISE # 4:

PLEASE COMPLETE AS MANY OF THESE STEPS AS POSSIBLE
DURING THE SMALL GROUP DISCUSSION TIMES. DUE TO
TIME CONSTRAINTS, YOU WILL NOT BE ABLE TO COMPLETE
ALL OF EXERCISE FOUR. HOWEVER, YOU CAN MAKE PLANS
FOR THE COMPLETION OF THIS LAST EXERCISE WITHIN THE
FRAMEWORK OF SMALL GROUP DISCUSSIONS.

The following is a ten-step program which, when applied properly,
helps us to understand the areas of our lives that require confession and
repentance. The Antidote of your life will be revealed if you have been
honest and faithful in this and the preceding three exercises.

In each of these steps, you will be asked to develop various goals. These
goals must be related to any specific scripting problem you may have. They
must be measurable. They must be attainable. And they must be subject to
a measurement in time. (They must be SMART goals!)

Step 1: Exploration and Discovery

What, if any, are the addictive elements of your life? What factors of
lost childhood are evident in your life?

What are the elements of your life that take an inordinate amount of
time? What can you not live without? Is there anything you hide from others,
some practice or habit? Addictions involve work, food, money, drugs, sex,
alcohol, anger, depression, anxiety, a person or a type of person, a behavior
pattern, caring for others, perfectionism, leisure, illness, a particular role
or roles, or any other addictive element of our lives. The addiction can
also involve our dedication to certain roles we are trying to re-create in
adulthood, such as an HP, a placator, etc. What did you enjoy doing as a
child? Can you recall instances of loss, gain, discipline or affection? These
are the keys to understanding the missing events of your childhood that
you may be looking for as an adult.

Tell the story of your life to a trusted friend or loved one, hopefully
someone within your small group. You may want to share this with a
counselor. This will help you to eliminate any areas of denial in your life.
Most importantly, tell your story to God. He already knows the addictive
elements of your life and wants you to be aware of them also. Allow your
small group members to tell you if they see any areas of denial.

Step 2: Relationship History

Identify everyone who has left a mark in your life, either positive or negative. Of course, consider your nuclear family, but also consider marriage partners, boyfriends or girlfriends, mentors, coaches, teachers, etc. If this step is done properly, recurring patterns will become apparent.

Share the results with a trusted friend or loved one, hopefully someone within your small group. You may want to share the results with a counselor. Share the results with God. The goal is to help you see the recurrent themes in your relationship history. Share these recurring patterns with your group. Allow the members of your small group to point out recurrent patterns that you may not have considered.

Step 3: Breaking the Addiction Cycle

The addictions in our lives, which we use to cover the pain of lost childhood and failed relationships, hypnotize us and prevent us from being able to see the causes of our failed relationships as well as our addictions. Addictions can also be called idols. They prevent us from focusing our attention on Christ. For this reason, no further steps can be pursued until the addictions of our lives are stopped. All addictions must be forsaken and eliminated. Addictions can be done to control others. Or they can be used to anesthetize against the pain that is in our lives. Addictions involve work, food, money, drugs, sex, alcohol, anger, depression, anxiety, a person or type of person, a behavior pattern, caring for others, perfectionism, leisure, illness, or any other addictive element of our lives. The addiction can also involve our dedication to certain roles we are trying to re-create in adulthood, like being a HP, a placator, etc. In some cases, the addiction must be broken immediately and decisively. In other cases, the addiction must be broken slowly through aversion therapy or other methods of desensitizing ourselves to the need for the addictive element. In many cases, effective boundaries must be set with those who enable or encourage our addictions. In extreme circumstances, separation from those who encourage or enable our addictions is necessary. In the case of marriage, if the individual who is encouraging or enabling the addiction is our mate, constructive plans for boundaries require careful consideration. The help of a professional Christian counselor is advised in any case in which escaping an addiction is something of a problem.

Confession and the exercise of the steps of The Antidote is now critical. Without confession of addictions to destructive roles and scripts, long term relational healing within any ministry structure will be difficult or even impossible (See 1 John 1:9).

Go back to exercises one through three and determine what compulsive behavior patterns you may have. Write a plan for breaking these addictions. Ask God for help in writing your plan. Remember, these goals must be related to your specific scripting problem. They must be measurable. They must be attainable. And they must be subject to a measurement in time. (They must be SMART goals!) Share these addictions and your plan for breaking these addictions with a trusted friend or loved one, hopefully someone within your small group. After making any changes to your plan as a result of the advice of the loved one or friend, submit your plan to your small group. Pray for guidance throughout the process. Ask your small group to help you refine your plan. Submit your plan to God. Once again, the help of a professional Christian counselor is advised in any case in which escaping an addiction is something of a problem.

Finally, put your plan into effect and ask the members of your small group to make you accountable to them in the implementation of your plan.

Step 4: Leaving Home and Saying Goodbye

When we have left our addictions, the real pain in our lives becomes exposed. No longer is there an anesthetic called addiction. At this point we can focus on leaving the problems of our childhood behind. In healthy families, this takes place naturally, in stages. We leave home physically, financially, and finally, emotionally. This does not mean we ever stop caring for our parents. However, it does mean that we stop looking to them for the emotional support we did not receive. It also means that we stop trying to give them the emotional support that children were not designed by God to give to their parents. It means that we stop depending on our parents financially when we have reached true adulthood. This ends the problem of re-creation as it ends the cycle of seeking the missing approval we did not receive from our parents. This is a painful step. It involves leaving comfortable patterns of relating to others in a dysfunctional way. The only real way of accomplishing this task is by transferring our needs to God. Without real security in Jesus, we will slip back into old patterns when times of stress or crisis arise. Design a plan for saying goodbye to your parents. This may be a real or a staged event. It is not done in hostility, but only in love. We are to put into place words such as these: "I'm going to be an adult and you are going to be an adult. I won't depend on you emotionally or financially." You may do this face to face, with your parents, or you may do it through a letter, or you may do it by talking to an empty chair. After designing your plan, submit it to a trusted friend or loved one, hopefully someone within your small group. Pray about your plan. Then, submit it to your entire small group for any further modification that may be needed. Ask your small group to keep you accountable in the implementation of your plan. If you find the implementation of your plan difficult, it is advised that you see a professional Christian counselor for help.

Step 5: Grief

As a result of the loss of an addiction, there is a need for grief. The addiction has been a friend, a factor that has allowed you to ignore the real problems of your life. When the addiction is gone, we face the real pain of our circumstance. Without Jesus to take the place of the addiction, we will return to old patterns when times of stress and strife come. We must give ourselves permission to grieve, to be depressed and process the loss. The steps in the grieving process are denial (we don't have to give up the addiction), anger (at the loss and the ones who are causing us to experience the loss), depression (if anger is not dealt with by suppression or repression), bargaining (asking God to stop the pain with some magical formula), sadness, and finally, resolution (the resolve to get through the process). And, once again, if considerable depression is experienced through this step or no grief is felt of any kind, it is advisable to see a professional Christian counselor.

Step 6: New Self-Perceptions

Nature abhors a vacuum. The empty spot that was filled with an addiction or a dysfunctional relationship must be filled with something else. Otherwise, a new addiction may develop. An exercise called free association can help to understand what we are fixated upon. This exercise must be done with the help of a trained Christian counselor. However, the only real solution is to fill our minds with dependence on Jesus. This can only be done through a consistent walk with Him.

Design a program for a regular Quiet Time with Jesus. This program should include Bible study, Bible memorization, and prayer. Ask the help of a trusted friend or loved one, one who is a mature Christian, and hopefully a member of your small group. Pray about your plan. Submit your plan to your entire small group. Ask your small group to give you any final modification that may be needed. Ask your small group to keep you accountable in the implementation of your plan.

Step 7: New Experiences

To support the new person that Christ is making us to be, we need to reinforce our dependence on Him. This comes through a support group of some kind made up of maturing Christians. This support group may or may not be the same small group that you have formed for this class as this process may take a considerable length of time. It also means that we need to develop habits of regular church attendance, listening to Christian music and being with other Christians.

Design a plan for developing new experiences. Ask the help of a trusted friend or loved one, hopefully a member of your small group. Pray about your plan. Submit your plan to your entire small group, whether this group is the one you formed for this class or one that consists of members of your church or ministry team. Ask your small group to give you any modification that may be needed. Ask your small group to keep you accountable in the implementation of your plan.

Step 8: Re-parenting

This is the task of finding someone to help us in the process of developing new self-perceptions and new experiences. This must not be a person who takes the place of an addictive relationship that was once a part of our lives. In this case, re-parenting would actually be re-creation. Rather, we must find a discipler, someone who has our best interest in mind, someone who will not tolerate our dependence on that person. This mentor must be one who will not involve us in any verbal, physical or sexual abuse. This person must not be involved in alcohol or drug use. This person must not be involved in any type of immorality. This person must not be involved in any illegal activities. This person must not possess the role of rescuer. This person must not take advantage of you in any way. In addition, this person must be one who will insist that you not be involved in any of the above activities.

Pray for a discipler. Ask God to lead you to someone who will not allow you to re-create the past through that person. Make a list of potential disciplers. Submit your list to a trusted friend or loved one. Continue praying about that person. Submit your list to your small group for modification or advice, whether this small group is the one you formed for this class or one that comes from your church or ministry team. Ask someone to be your discipler. If that person is not interested, keep searching for God's will in this area of your life until someone agrees to help you. Give the results of the four exercises of this course to that person. Ask for that person's help in maintaining the steps you have taken.

Step 9: Relationship Accountability

At the first sign of any re-creation between you and anyone else, break the relationship. Ask your discipler to help you in seeing if re-creation is occurring between you and another. Ask a second person, a trusted friend or loved one, to help you monitor the situation between you and your discipler. If you are developing a re-creational relationship with your discipler, break that relationship and find another discipler.

Step 10: Maintenance

Write out the script of your life that you have discovered through these exercises. Develop a daily program of refusing to be involved in any of these scripted activities. Maintain a daily Quiet Time. Periodically review these ten steps. Submit this plan to a trusted friend or loved one and to your group, whether the group formed for this class or a group that is part of your church or ministry team. And, submit this plan to your discipler

Local Church Survey

The following pages contain a survey that can be conducted in a local church. The purpose of this survey is to give an analysis of a church's potential or actual condition. The survey is subjective. Standards for the local church regarding totals for survey answers have not been developed. It is only designed to be used as a tool for a pastor or church advisor in the task of analyzing a local church.

Appendix

Analyzing your Church

Answer each question with a number between 1 and 5 with these criteria in mind:

1=never   2=seldom   3=unknown or not applicable 4=occasionally 5=frequently

1._____Does your church have a history of conflict?

2._____Do people in your church steadfastly state that there is no conflict within your church?

3._____Do non-member, attenders of your church think the church has too much conflict?

4._____Do community members around your church think the church has too much conflict?

5._____Is there any evidence of problems toward pastoral authority within the behavior of staff or lay leaders within your church?

6._____Is there a laziness or competency issue with any staff or lay leaders of your church?

7._____Is the pastor given a formal review, written or otherwise, from laymen in your church?

8._____Is the pastor given a formal review, written or otherwise, from leaders within your church who may not actually have a ministry in ministering the Word of God?

9._____Is your church known for unharmonious relationships between the pastor and the leadership board?

10._____Do any former pastors or former interim pastors of your church or denominational officials attempt to influence your church while being a part of the church?

11._____Are charges against your pastor tolerated with less than two or three actual witnesses (those who have actually seen the sin)?

12._____Are charges against your pastor tolerated that are not actual Biblical sins?

13._____Is there any open hostility between members of your church?

14._____When discipline is necessary, does your church tend to disregard the procedures of Matthew 18:15-20 and 1 Timothy 5:19-20?

15._____Is your church in danger of families leaving the church at this time?

16._____Have any of the last few pastors at your church stayed less than five years?

17._____Has a pastor ever been dismissed or forced to resign from your church?

18._____Has more than one pastor ever been dismissed or forced to resign from your church?

19._____Does your church fail to hire an interim pastor when there is a pastoral vacancy?

20._____Is there a definite group which is in control or wishes to be in control within your church?

21._____Is there a refusal or resistance on the part of a group within your church to accept examination or outside help when conflict occurs?

22._____Is there someone or a group of people within your church who always insist that others are the problem when conflict occurs?

23._____Is there a particular person or a group of people who always seems to be involved in church problems within your church?

24._____Is there evidence of personal family or business failures on the part of your church's senior board leaders?

25._____Is there any evidence of a lie being told by any church leader or staff member?

26._____Are there secret meetings within your church either by the senior board or unrecognized groups?

27._____Are attacks on others, staff or laymen, evident within your church?

28._____Are there examples of extreme childhood trauma in the background of leaders or staff members within your church?

29._____Are there several unique cultural subgroups within your church?

30._____Can a person known for his or her ability to solve problems be identified within your church?

31._____If you have a person who is known for identifying problems, is that person good at pointing out the failures of others while not noting their own failures or the failures of their own particular group?

32._____Is there someone within your church who is known to seek out meetings with key leaders or the pastor?

33._____Is there someone who likes to meet with pastoral candidates during their time of candidacy at your church?

34._____Is your church known for being somewhat stagnant in growth?

35._____Has conflict been evident during any time that your church has been in a positive growth cycle?

36._____In the past, have charges against the pastor been investigated without the correction of either the pastor or the accuser being completed?

37._____Do your church leaders find it difficult to confess either their own personal sins or corporate sins within the leadership team?

38._____Do your leaders resist the suggestion of outside help when conflict occurs?

39._____Are you aware of any leader or participant in conflict telling a lie in your church?

40._____Does your church fail to fully qualify senior leadership board members Biblically (see 1 Timothy 3:1-7, 5:17-25 and Titus 1:6-9 if necessary)?

41._____Do any of your senior board church leaders fail to serve in a ministry function which ministers the Word?

42._____Does doing this survey offend you or others within your church?

43._____Does your church have non-elected leaders or those not properly appointed by the pastor and the senior board?

44._____Have any of your church's leaders resigned in the last five years rather than completing their term for reasons other than a physical move or some other understandable reason?

45._____Are leadership board meetings dominated by problems and disciplinary matters?

46._____Has your church failed to have a clear vision statement?

47._____Is there ever open hostility voiced at congregational meetings of your church?

48._____Is there ever open hostility voiced at senior board meetings of your church?

49._____Has your church failed to have 5% growth rate by evangelism during each of the last five years?

50._____If you are in a pastoral search process, is there a person or persons who dominate the pastoral search process?

Please add the numbers for each of your answers. What is your total?____

Please record the question numbers in which you scored an answer of 5:

_____

Please record the question numbers in which you scored an answer of 4:

_____